100 great recipes

Meals in Minutes

100 great recipes
Meals in Minutes

Ann Nicol

FALL RIVER PRESS

Previously published by D&S with ISBN: 978-0-7607-8100-5

This 2009 edition published by Fall River Press,
by arrangement with Kerswell Books Ltd,
under license from Kerswell Farm Ltd

Creative Director: Sarah King
Editor: Debbie Key
Project Editor: Nicola Barber
Photography: Colin Bowling/Paul Forrester
Design: Axis Design

Fall River Press
122 Fifth Avenue
New York, NY 10011

ISBN: 978-1-4351-1629-0

Printed and bound in China

10 9 8 7 6 5 4 3 2 1

Contents

Introduction 6

Fast Food can be Good Food 9

Planning 11

Pantry Basics 12

Freezer Basics 14

Fridge Basics 17

Vegetable-bin Basics 17

Herbs 18

Cook's Tips 20

Cook's Tools 22

Fast Ways of Cooking 24

Microwaving 26

Tips for Successful Cooking 31

Family Meals 36

Light Meals 78

Vegetarian Meals 120

Entertaining 166

Desserts 212

Index 254

Credits and Acknowledgements 256

Introduction

People seem to have less and less time to spare these days, particularly for cooking. More people are struggling to combine a full-time job with running a home and raising children, and today's busy lifestyles just don't allow for hours spent in the kitchen preparing and cooking food. *Meals in Minutes* has therefore been aimed specifically at those who want to cook in a hurry, but who nevertheless still want to prepare delicious, healthy, and attractive-looking food for themselves and their families.

Meals in Minutes contains a collection of recipes, ranging from those for family meals to ones for impressive supper-party dishes, and including recipes for light meals, vegetarian meals, and desserts. These dishes can all be prepared quickly and cooked in 30 minutes or less. On the following pages, you'll also find helpful advice on planning, time-saving tips, and suggestions on how to fit shopping, food-preparation, and cooking into a busy schedule. In this way, *Meals in Minutes* will show you how to make the time to produce attractive and nutritious meals, whatever the occasion.

The family-meals section comprises a collection of recipes for substantial dishes for midweek meals, which have been designed for either two people eating together or a larger family of four sharing a meal. The light-meals recipes are particularly suitable for quick lunches and suppers, and may also be ideal for teenagers who don't want to stick to regular mealtimes and tend to graze whenever they feel hungry. Vegetarian cooking has grown ever more popular, and is also a popular style of eating with teenagers, which is why I have included a section that provides recipes for delicious and nourishing, meat-free meals that will appeal to all members of the family. Inviting friends to share a meal with you is one of life's pleasures, and shouldn't be neglected just because you feel that you don't have the time to cook at the end of a busy working day. The section aimed at entertaining shows how little extra effort is involved in cooking for special occasions, giving you more time to spend with your friends and less in the kitchen. Finally, most of us love to finish off a meal with a tempting dessert, and you'll find that the dishes in this section are simple to prepare and make, as well as being colorful and tasty.

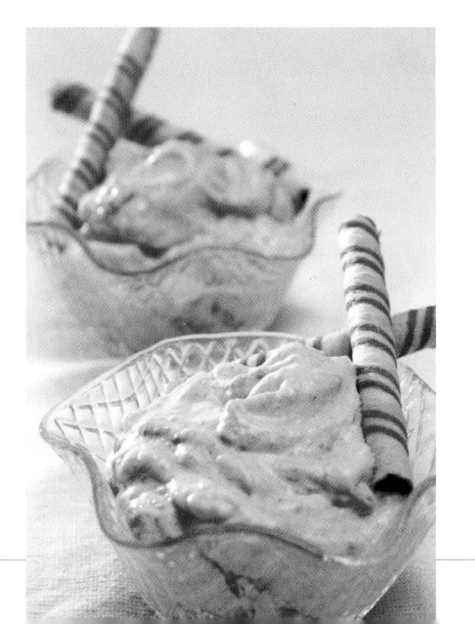

Even in today's busy world, it is still possible to cook up a delicious meal in the time that it takes to reheat a shop-bought, ready-made meal. All that is required is a little organization. Buy fresh foods when you have the time, but plan to have a supply of convenience foods to hand with which to supplement them. And for those days when it is not easy to buy fresh ingredients, you will be able to rely on the stock that you have squirreled away in your freezer and pantry.

Fast Food can be Good Food

Quickly cooked food not only gives you more time to spend on other activities, it can be healthy food, too. Commercially manufactured, ready-made meals may be the wrong type of convenience food as they can be full of hidden fats, colorings, and preservatives. There is an abundance of convenience foods that you can combine with fresh foods to produce healthy meals, however, so don't feel guilty about using canned, dried and frozen foods because these can still supply the essential nutrients that your family needs.

Fresh Foods can be Economical

You'll soon discover that you don't have to spend a great deal of money in order to eat quick and healthy meals. Dollar for dollar, buying and cooking fresh foods is the surest way of maintaining your family's health. You'll probably find that bought, ready-made meals cost at least double the price of the fresh, raw ingredients which can be cooked in about the same time that it takes to heat up a bought product.

Know What you are Eating

If you want to know what's in your food, then it's always worth taking the time to cook from scratch. Preparing meals at home means that you have control over everything that goes into them, and that you can cut down on the amount of fats and additives that they contain. You'll also find that cooking foods quickly reduces the amount of time that they are exposed to heat, thereby conserving valuable nutritional components.

Maintain a Healthy Balance

The recipes in this book have been planned with nutritional balance in mind to help you and your family to maintain a healthy diet. Adding fresh vegetables, fruit, and healthy ingredients to those that you take from a well-stocked fridge or panry makes for a good nutritional balance, and also helps you to create dishes quickly and easily.

The amount of salt included in these recipes has been left to your personal preference, but note that it is healthier to reduce your salt consumption, so try to add as little salt as possible when cooking and seasoning, particularly if salty foods, such as bacon, are included in the list of ingredients.

Planning

If you are organized, and have a well-stocked kitchen, you will easily be able to cope with such unexpected situations as leaving the office late or having extra friends for dinner. Emergencies need never be a disaster if you have a plan, so that you won't have to spend all night in the kitchen or waste valuable time shopping on the way home, when you may end up buying the last, wilting vegetables at extortionate prices from the local store.

The secret of successful, fast cooking is good organization. With some simple planning, you can save time on shopping trips, while time spent in the kitchen will be a pleasure rather than a chore.

Shopping and Stocking up

One of the best ways to ensure that you can cook a week's meals is to plan your shopping when you have the time. Here are some other time-saving tips.

- Planned meals are much more economical than unplanned ones, so keep a list in a notebook, or on a piece of paper, of the stocks that are running low in your pantry.

- Make sure that you have a supply of plastic wrap, aluminum foil, parchment paper and strong freezer bags for the freezer.

- Always make a list before going shopping. This way, you won't forget vital ingredients.

- When you have time, do a big shop once a month. If you are shopping at the weekend, try to go early in the morning, when the stores are not so busy, and then stock up on all of the basics.

- Stock up on items with a long shelf-life, such as canned food or pasta, when they are on special offer.

Pantry Basics

The foods in your pantry will no doubt reflect your personal preferences, but you'll find that keeping the following basic foods to hand will help you to rustle up tasty meals in no time at all.

Cans and Longlife Foods

Keep a stock of the following canned and long-life foods:

- canned fish, such as tuna, salmon, mackerel fillets, and anchovies;

- canned vegetables, such as tomatoes, pimentos, corn, asparagus tips, and a wide variety of beans and legumes like lima beans, garbanzos, cannellini, and red kidney beans;

- canned fruits, such as pears, apricots, and peaches;

- longlife milk and powdered, sweetened condensed, and evaporated milk.

Dried Foods

Keep a good store of the following dried foods in your pantry:

- packs of easy-cook, risotto, and long-grain rice;

- a variety of pasta shells, bows, tubes, and ribbons;

- Dried herbs and spices (which always help to liven up dishes, see page 22).

Bottles and Jars

Stock up on the following bottled products.

- Artichoke hearts in oil. Artichoke hearts make a quick, salad-type meal, and you can sprinkle the oil over the dish.

- Capers, which are sold in brine in jars, or else salted and dry. These can be chopped and added to dishes to give them extra piquancy.

- Bottled fruits, such as morello and black cherries. These make delicious, quick desserts when teamed with ice cream.

- Different types of oils and vinegars. Keep a selection of olive, sunflower, and sesame-seed oils, for example, for cooking and flavoring foods. Red- and white-wine vinegars are good basics, but adding sherry and balsamic vinegars to your store cupboard will give you more versatility when it comes to making delicious dressings and sauces.

- Tubes of tomato paste and plastic bottles of tomato ketchup. These are not only handy, but you can squeeze out exactly the right amount required.

- Jars of green-basil and red pesto. These are useful for adding to sauces or for topping meats before broiling.

Freezer Basics

A well-stocked freezer will really help to save you time, and can also supply a meal when you have no time for shopping. Keep the following basic foods in your freezer.

Bread

You need not buy fresh bread on the way home if you keep a supply of sliced bread or speciality bread and rolls like ciabatta in the freezer. Frozen crusty and sliced bread, rolls, and pizza bases can go straight into the oven without being defrosted, and part-baked bread can similarly be heated through in the oven while you are preparing a soup or a salad.

Cheese

Frozen, grated cheese can be used for toppings without being defrosted first. Freeze small batches of grated cheese in plastic bags or boxes so it can be ready to sprinkle over hot dishes and melted under the broiler.

Chicken

Chicken portions, such as breasts, thighs, and drumsticks, are very useful food items to keep in the freezer, but remember that they must be completely thawed before being cooked. Cut a whole bird into evenly sized pieces, or pack fresh joints in the freezer by separating them with freezer paper, so that individual portions can easily be removed and defrosted. Cooked chicken can also be stored in the freezer: after cooking, cool it quickly, then slice it or take it off the bone and interleave the pieces with aluminum foil or freezer paper before freezing in strong plastic bags or boxes.

Cream and Ice Cream

Buy packs of frozen cream, sold in small, individual blocks. These can be quickly defrosted for pouring or whipping and allow you to use the exact amount you need. A tub of ice cream is a good standby for serving with fruit salads and canned fruits.

Dough, Pastry, and Pastry Shells

Keep a frozen, unbaked pastry shell in a baking tin in the freezer ready to make into a tart or quiche. Frozen, ready-rolled, puff pastry and phyllo leaves can be part-thawed quickly and easily unrolled to bake into desserts.

Fish Fillets and Steaks

Bags of individually frozen pieces of fish are sold in supermarkets, and these are invaluable for keeping in the freezer. Just remove the amount required for a recipe and reseal the bag.

Fruits

Frozen fruits such as raspberries, blueberries and black currants will thaw quickly to make desserts.

Herbs

Frozen herbs have a far superior flavor to dried ones, and are almost comparable to fresh ones in this respect. Frozen herbs can be bought in small tubs and can then be kept in the freezer for crumbling directly into sauces or over dishes. Home-grown herbs can either be packed into freezer bags and frozen on their stems or else be chopped before being bagged and frozen, enabling you to remove teaspoonfuls from the freezer bag as and when you need them. (See also page 22.)

Shrimp

Cooked, frozen shrimp are great for using straight from the freezer. If they are small, rinse them in a colander under lukewarm water, but if they are larger, defrost them in the microwave oven (see page 30) and then pat them dry with paper towels. Large, gray, part-thawed, uncooked shrimp can be cooked through until they turn pink.

Link Sausages, Chops and Ground Meat

Pork link sausages and pork and lamb chops freeze extremely well. Note that for quick defrosting, it is best to freeze ground beef, lamb, and pork in small batches. If you are freezing them raw, separate the chops and link sausages and either wrap them individually in freezer wrap before packing them into strong freezer bags, or else pack them into freezer bags in

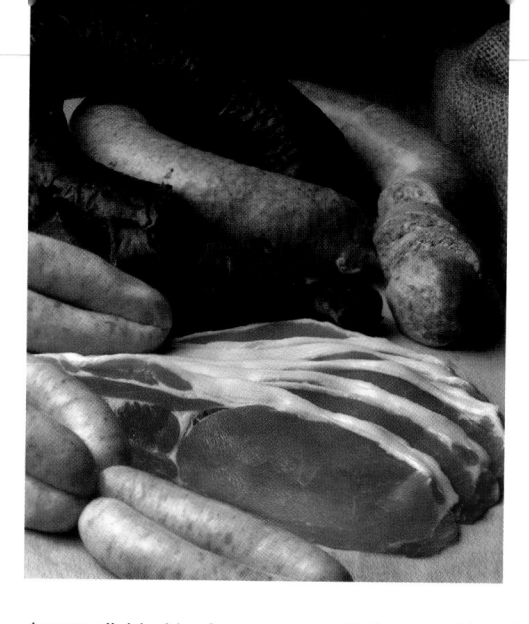

layers divided by freezer wrap. Before cooking them in the evening, either remove them from the freezer in the morning and leave them to defrost in the fridge all day, or else defrost small batches at a time in the microwave oven (see page 30).

vegetables

Frozen vegetables can be cooked straight from the freezer in minutes in the microwave oven or on the cooktop. Keep a stock of frozen peas, fava beans, spinach, and corn in the freezer with which to add color and flavor to many quick dishes.

Fridge Basics

Stock your fridge with these basics:

- butter;
- bacon (bacon, Canadian bacon, lard leaves or pancetta);
- cheese (Cheddar cheese, Parmesan cheese, feta cheese, mozzarella and goat cheese);
- eggs;
- ham;
- mayonnaise;
- olives;
- salads and salad vegetables;
- pepperoni, salami, or chorizo sausage.

Vegetable-bin Basics

The following vegetable-bin basics will keep well in a cool, dry place:

- carrots;
- garlic;
- onions and shallots;
- potatoes.

Herbs

When there is little time to develop the flavors of foods through slow cooking, fresh herbs will add an appetising tang. Don't worry that using a herb will spoil the taste of a dish because you'll find that the right one will complement the flavors of other ingredients: basil, for example, will enhance the taste of tomatoes.

Cook's Tip: Dried Herbs
If you cannot find a particular fresh herb, either replace it with a dried one (use half the specified amount) or else use a puréed or frozen herb instead.

Basil is an extremely versatile herb, with a warm, spicy flavor. Its leaves blend to best effect with tomatoes, either raw or cooked, in pasta sauces or cheese dishes. The flavor of basil also works well with garlic and wine-based sauces.

Bay leaves blend well with meats, such as lamb and poultry.

Chives have delicate, onion-flavored leaves which are best used raw or added at the end of the cooking time. Chives are ideal for garnishing, particularly egg, cheese, and poultry dishes.

Cilantro has a distinctively fresh, earthy flavor, and is mainly used in Oriental dishes. To appreciate its concentrated flavor at its best, chop it up and sprinkle it over a dish just before serving.

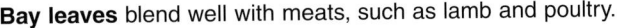

Cumin seeds are used whole or ground and have a slightly perfumed quality. They contribute a lively flavor when cooked in lamb, chicken, and vegetable dishes.

Garlic is one of the most widely used flavorings. Crush or chop it before adding it to sauces and dishes to liven them up and add depth and warmth.

Marjoram and oregano are small, green, delicately scented leaves that are used in vegetarian dishes, many pasta sauces, and Mediterranean dishes.

Mint is a refreshing leaf, with a distinctive flavor, that is widely teamed with lamb or used as a garnish.

Parsley is probably the most commonly used herb for cooking, and is best either added to dishes raw or, in the case of fish and egg dishes, at the end of the cooking time. Italian parsley has a stronger flavor than the curly variety.

Rosemary is a pungent herb, so use it sparingly or its powerful flavor can take over. It combines well with lamb and pork.

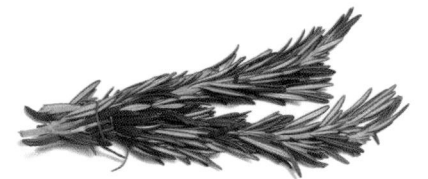

Thyme has a strong flavor that especially complements garlic, tomatoes, onions, fish, seafood, and chicken.

Have everything that you need to hand

Cook's Tips

To avoid wasting time in the kitchen, follow these handy tips.

- Keep a list of essential pantry items and highlight them when they are running low so that you don't run out of them.

- Make sure that you have all of the ingredients that you will need before starting cooking, then you won't get halfway through a recipe and find that you don't have a vital ingredient, or that it needs defrosting.

- A tidy kitchen and working space will help you to cook quickly. Uncluttered cupboards will help you to locate ingredients rapidly, and because working in a cluttered environment slows down cooking, throw waste and empty packaging into the garbage as you work.

- Make the most of your food processor and keep it handy on a work surface rather than stowing it away in a closet.

- Before you begin to prepare the food, read through the recipe and become familiar with the method so that you can easily follow the steps while you are cooking.

- Make sure that you have all your ingredients and equipment to hand before starting to cook.

- Your oven may take between 10 and 15 minutes to heat up, so if you are using it, turn it on first, before starting to prepare your ingredients. (Electric convection ovens don't usually have to be preheated, but check the manufacturer's instructions.)

- Broilers need to be properly preheated before use. For fast and even cooking, keep the broiler set to high to avoid any uncooked patches of food. Regularly check tender foods, such as fish, for burning or lower the broiler pan a few notches down from the heat source.

- Use the microwave oven for small, quick jobs, such as melting butter and chocolate, heating all-in-one sauces, defrosting, thawing, and reheating. Use it for cooking potatoes, scrambled eggs, and frozen vegetables, such as peas, quickly.

- If boiling water is required, switch on the teakettle or boil a pan of water in advance.

- Plan your cooking so that you can do two things at once: start the water boiling for pasta while you sauté chopped onions for a sauce, for instance.

- Warm serving bowls and dishes quickly by placing them in the sink, draining the hot water in which you cooked pasta or vegetables over them and then wiping them dry before use.

Keep your food processor where it's easily accessible

Read through the whole recipe before you begin

Cook's Tools

You'll find the following tools a great help in preparing meals in minutes.

Tools for Measuring, Cutting, Chopping, and Grating

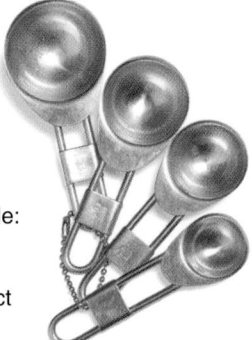

Keeping the following small items in a kitchen drawer will prove invaluable:

Cook's measures A set of spoons or cups will help you to use the exact amounts that a recipe requires.

Graters Hand-held graters with a handle make fast work of small items. Lemon zest, cheese, or such fats as butter can be grated directly into sauces.

Kitchen scissors Kitchen scissors are indispensable for fast cooking. Use them for snipping foods directly into the pan instead of getting out your chopping board and kitchen knives.

Knives Make sure that you have a basic set of three or four good-quality, sharp kitchen knives.

Vegetable-peeler A swivel-headed vegetable-peeler can be used for quickly cutting vegetables such as potatoes, carrots, and zucchini into ribbonlike strips. It is also good for making large curls of Parmesan cheese and chocolate.

Pans Use pans that are the right size for the job and the ingredients. You don't need to boil a large pan of water to cook a small quantity of vegetables, for instance.

Skillets When browning meat, it is best to use a large skillet. In a small one, the pieces of meat will be too close together, so that rather than dry-frying, they will produce steam.

Au gratin dishes Metal au gratin dishes are better than porcelain ones because they conduct heat more quickly and evenly, thus reducing cooking times.

Pasta pans You will need a large pan for cooking pasta because it will cook more quickly in plenty of water. A pasta pan with a separate strainer basket that lifts out makes draining the pasta easier than tipping it into a colander or sieve.

A wok A wok can be used as a large skillet for stir-frying, and, if it has a lid, it can also double up as a steamer.

Electric kitchen aids Electric food processors and hand-held blenders can really save you time in the kitchen.

Food processors Food processors are designed for chopping, grating, and shredding in seconds. They have a selection of blades that speed up the process of shredding vegetables, grating cheese and chopping meats, vegetables, and herbs, and can also make breadcrumbs for toppings superquickly. They will beat and blend mixtures much more rapidly than is possible by hand, too.

Hand-held food blenders Hand-held food blenders are useful for quickly making sauces and easily blending lumps out of sauces that have gone wrong. They can also quickly make purées and can purée soups while still in the pan.

Fast Ways of Cooking

Many time-saving techniques can speed up your food preparation and cooking. For fast results, follow these techniques.

Chopping and Slicing

Save time by following these chopping and slicing tips.

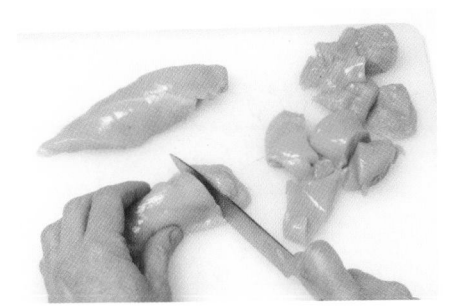

- Cut vegetables and meats into small, even pieces or thin slices to speed up their cooking time.

- Use kitchen scissors for snipping up bacon and ham rather than using a knife. You can also snip green onions and fresh herbs directly into, or over, dishes.

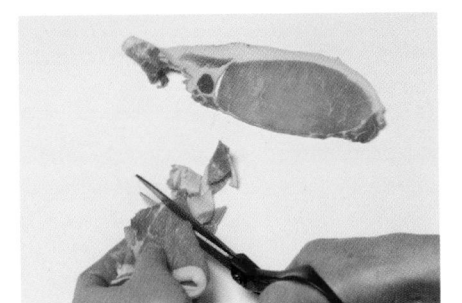

- Save on dish-washing time by using your clean hands to crumble cheese, tear up lettuce leaves or perform quick jobs like flaking fish.

Boiling

If boiling is required, you may find these tips useful.

- Vegetables will cook much quicker if arranged in a shallow layer in a large pan than in a deep layer in a small one.

- A large pan filled with boiling water will cook pasta more quickly than a small one. Speed things along by heating half of the water in the teakettle first.

- Heat stocks and sauces before you need them and then simmer them to keep them warm.

Frying and Broiling

When frying or broiling, remember the following tips.

- Cut or slice meat or vegetables into equal-sized pieces of the same thickness so that they cook at the same rate.

- Speed up the time that burgers and patties take to cook by forming them into thin, flat shapes.

- For fast, even cooking, preheat the broiler thoroughly.

Microwaving

A versatile time-saver, the microwave oven is invaluable when it comes to everyday cooking. It not only speeds up the thawing of frozen foods, but helps with food preparation and cooking. The microwave oven cooks in minutes, and anyone who owns a microwave oven knows that they are safe, economical, time-saving, and very easy to use.

The basic principle of microwave cooking is that food is cooked by the action of microwaves on water molecules. Microwaves pass directly through cooking containers into food, metal being the only substance with which this process does not work as it reflects the microwaves, making it impossible for them to reach the food.

The microwave oven cannot completely replace conventional cooking because there are some things that it simply cannot do, such as deep-frying, cooking tougher meats, and boiling eggs (which will explode in the microwave). Food cooked in microwaves does not brown in the conventional way.

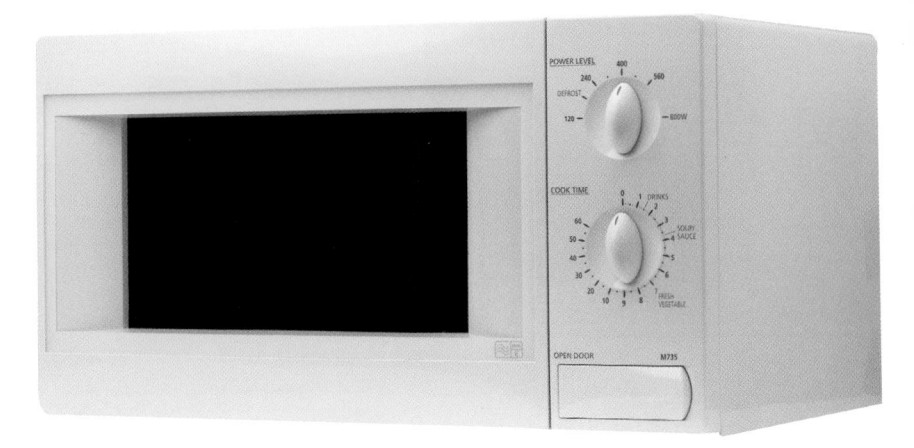

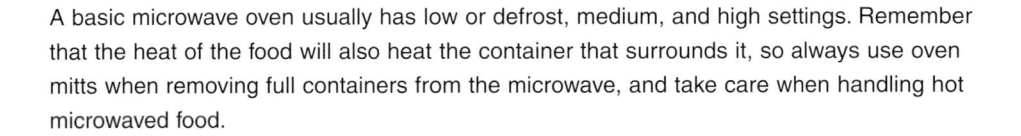

A basic microwave oven usually has low or defrost, medium, and high settings. Remember that the heat of the food will also heat the container that surrounds it, so always use oven mitts when removing full containers from the microwave, and take care when handling hot microwaved food.

Don't use any metal dishes in your microwave oven, or any container that has a metal trim or handles. Don't use lead crystal in the microwave either, and remember that the heat of the foods that they contain will cause thin, plastic containers such as ice-cream tubs to distort, which is why you should instead use rigid, plastic containers that have been designed for microwaving.

Cook's Tip: Quantities and Timings

Although cooking in a microwave speeds up preparation and cooking times dramatically, remember that unlike using a conventional cooker, if you double the amount of ingredients, the cooking time must be doubled, too.

Microwave Shortcuts

If you have a microwave oven, you'll find these short cuts invaluable.

- Soften butter from the fridge by warming it for 20 seconds on medium.

- To melt chocolate, break it into small pieces and place them in a bowl. Transfer the uncovered bowl to the microwave and melt the chocolate on low or medium, taking the bowl out of the microwave every 10 seconds or so to stir and check the chocolate to ensure that it does not overcook and seize.

- Cook poppadoms one at a time for 40 seconds on high until they puff up.

- Cook bacon by arranging three slices at a time, without overlapping them, on a paper towel. Cover the slices with another paper towel and cook on high for 1½ to 2 minutes. Then leave to stand for 4 minutes.

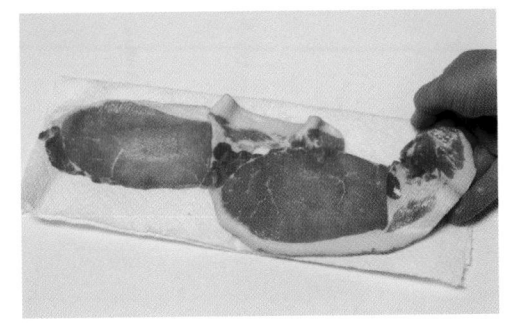

Cook's Tip: Standing Time

Don't forget that food continues to cook after it has been taken out of the microwave. During the standing time, the residual heat in the food will complete the cooking process, so follow any cooking instructions carefully.

Defrosting

Microwaves can speed up defrosting times considerably, particularly if the following tips are heeded.

- Always underestimate defrosting times, and stop defrosting if the food feels warm.

- Small amounts or blocks of frozen food will defrost more quickly than larger ones.

- If food is in an aluminum-foil container, transfer it to a microwave-proof dish instead. Also remove any metal tags.

- Cover foods like stews and vegetables with a plate or plastic wrap to speed up the defrosting process.

- Cover such foods as bread, pasties and cakes with paper towels to absorb any moisture and prevent them from becoming soggy while thawing.

- When a recipe states "cover," use either the lid provided with the microwave container or place a plate or some plastic wrap over the dish.

- When using plastic wrap, make sure that it does not come into direct contact with the food and pierce it in one or two places with a small knife to allow the steam to escape and prevent the plastic wrap from ballooning in the heat. After cooking, peel back the plastic wrap from the far side of the dish to prevent the danger of the steam rushing out and burning you.

- Break up such foods as ground beef or soup with a spoon as they begin to soften. Remove the bowl from the microwave and mash the food with a spoon.

Quick Microwave Ways with Potatoes

Potatoes usually take some time to cook by conventional means, which is one of the reasons why a microwave oven is a real boon when time is short.

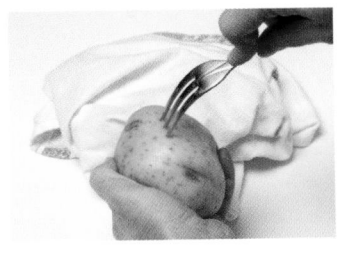

Baked Potatoes

Buy large, oval-shaped, old potatoes weighing about 7oz each. Don't peel them, just scrub them under cold, running water, pat them dry, and pierce the skins several times with a fork. Rub the skins with a little butter and salt and arrange the potatoes in a circle on a piece of kitchen paper on the microwave's turntable.

Now cook the potatoes on high (100 percent power) for 7 to 8 minutes for two servings, or 14 to 15 minutes for four servings, turning the potatoes over halfway through the cooking time (remember to turn the microwave off before doing this).

Carefully wrap the potatoes in a clean dish towel and let them stand for 5 minutes before serving them. (The potatoes are done if they are tender when squeezed, but be careful not to burn your fingers while doing so.)

New Potatoes

Choose evenly sized new potatoes, but if some are larger, cut them in half. Scrub the potatoes thoroughly, but don't peel away their skins. Pierce each potato once with a fork. Allowing 8oz for 2 people, and 1lb for 4 people, arrange the potatoes around the edge of a shallow, 8½in, round, microwave-proof dish. Add 2 (4) tablespoons of water to the bowl, cover and cook for 3 to 4 (6 to 7) minutes on high.

Leave the potatoes to stand for 5 minutes, still covered. They should be tender when pierced with the point of a knife before serving.

Sliced Potatoes

Scrub old potatoes under cold water and then cut them (unpeeled) into ¼in-thick slices, allowing 8oz for 2 people and 1lb for 4 people. Place the slices in a shallow, 8in, microwave-proof baking dish, arranging the larger slices towards the edges. Add ½ cup of water and cook on high for 4 (8) minutes, or until the potatoes are tender.

Drain and serve the sliced potatoes, either alone or covered with a cheese sauce or grated-cheese topping.

Tips for Successful Cooking

- Use measuring spoons and cups.
- All spoon measurements are level unless otherwise stated.
- All eggs are medium unless otherwise stated.
- Recipes using raw or lightly cooked eggs should not be given to babies, pregnant women, the very old, or anyone suffering from, or recovering from an illness.
- The cooking times are an approximate guide only. If you are using a convection oven reduce the cooking time according to the manufacturer's instructions.
- Ovens should be preheated to the required temperature.
- Fruits and vegetables should be washed before use.

Servings

Most of the recipes list ingredients for 2 and 4 servings. If, in the instructions, you see one quantity following another in brackets (2 (4) tablespoons, for example), the first figure is applicable if you are serving 2, and the second, if you are serving 4.

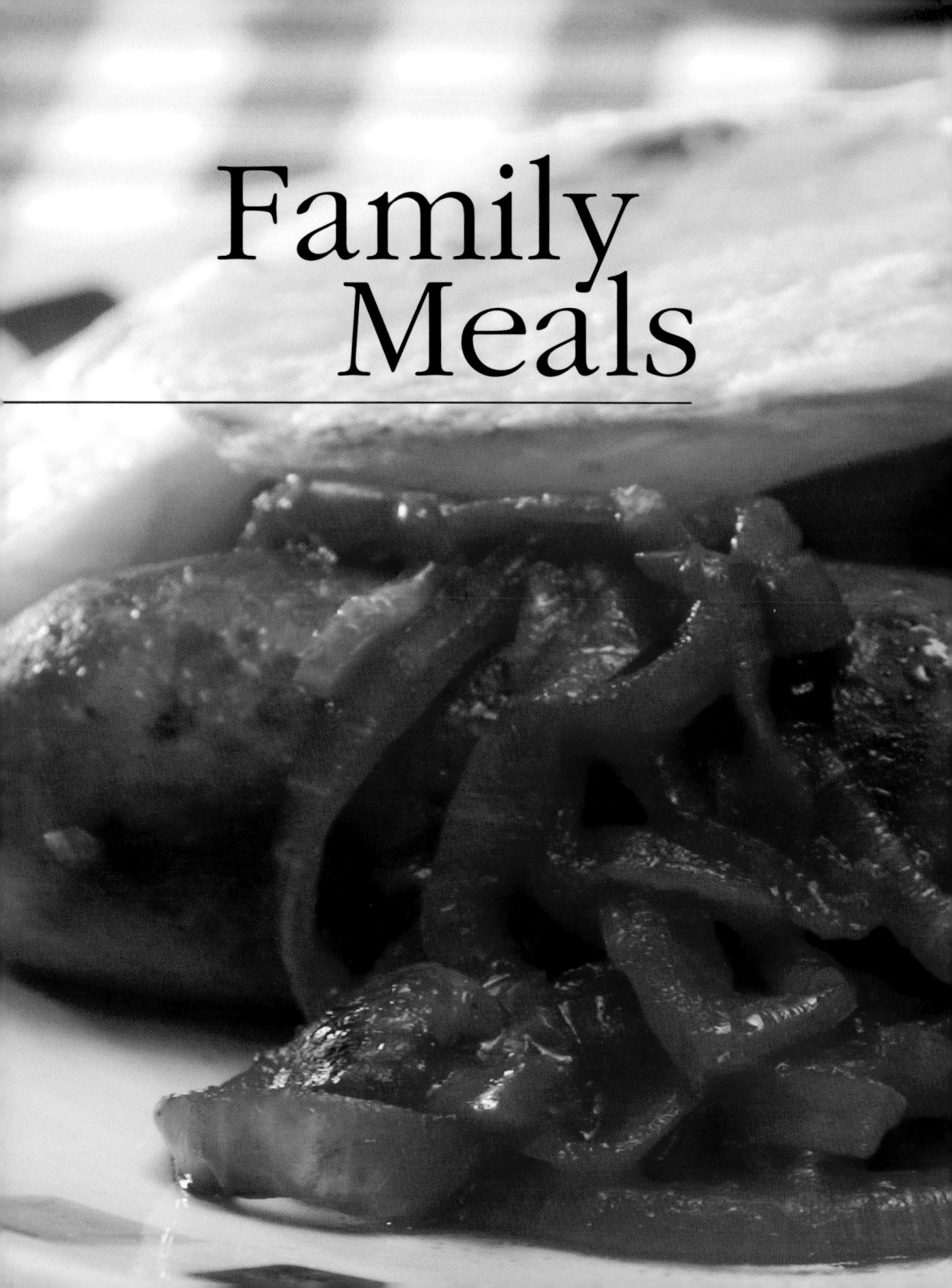

Family
Meals

Spicy Chicken Broil

spicy

Combine fresh chicken breasts with ingredients from the pantry for a quick, tasty supper.

Ingredients for 2

- **2 tsp medium curry paste**
- **1 tbsp mango chutney, chopped**
- **1 tbsp sunflower oil**
- **12oz skinless and boneless chicken-breast fillets**
- **¾ cup quick-cook couscous**
- **1½ tsp unsalted butter**
- **salt**
- **black pepper, freshly ground**
- **1 tbsp fresh cilantro, chopped**
- **1 ripe tomato, finely diced**
- **2 tbsp thick Greek-style yogurt**

Ingredients for 4

- **1 tbsp medium curry paste**
- **2 tbsp mango chutney, chopped**
- **2 tbsp sunflower oil**
- **1¼lb skinless and boneless chicken-breast fillets**
- **1½ cups quick-cook couscous**
- **1 tbsp unsalted butter**
- **salt**
- **black pepper, freshly ground**
- **2 tbsp fresh cilantro, chopped**
- **2 ripe tomatoes, finely diced**
- **4 tbsp thick Greek-style yogurt**

10 minutes preparation
15 minutes cooking

1 Mix the curry paste, chutney, and oil together in a bowl. Cut the chicken fillets in half and stir to coat in the mixture.

2 Line a broiler pan with aluminum foil and heat to high. Place the chicken pieces on the aluminum foil and broil for about 10 minutes, turning over once, until golden.

3 Meanwhile, make up the couscous with boiling water according to the package instructions, (it should take 10–15 minutes). When the couscous has soaked up all the water, stir in the butter, fluff it up with a fork and season with salt and pepper.

4 Spoon the couscous into a bowl and fold in the cilantro and diced tomatoes. Serve the chicken fillets with the couscous and 1 tablespoon each of thick, Greek-style yogurt.

Liver & Bacon Stir-fry

Quick and Easy

Liver and bacon must be the quickest stir-fry ever. Be careful not to overcook the liver, however, as it will become hard and tough.

Ingredients for 2

1 tbsp all-purpose flour
salt
black pepper, freshly ground
8oz lamb liver
1 tbsp sunflower oil
4 slices smoked bacon, rinds removed and chopped
1 medium onion, sliced into rings
2oz cremini or white mushrooms, sliced
1 tsp soy sauce

Ingredients for 4

2 tbsp all-purpose flour
salt
black pepper, freshly ground
1lb lamb liver
2 tbsp sunflower oil
8 slices smoked bacon, rinds removed and chopped
1 large onion, sliced into rings
4oz cremini or white mushrooms, sliced
2 tsp soy sauce

10 minutes preparation
10 minutes cooking

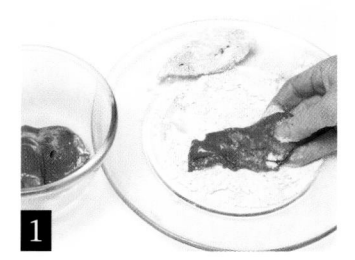

1 Spread the flour on a plate and season with salt and freshly ground black pepper. Cut the liver into thin slices, removing any pieces of skin or membrane, then dust the liver lightly in the flour.

2 Heat the oil in a large nonstick skillet or wok and fry the bacon and onion for 4 minutes until the fat runs from the bacon and the onion is softened and browned.

3 Add the mushrooms and cook over a medium heat for a further 2 minutes, stirring constantly.

4 Add the sliced liver and cook until the outside is browned and the inside is just cooked, for about 2–3 minutes. The liver should be slightly pink inside, (be careful not to overcook it as it will become tough.) Sprinkle with soy sauce and serve immediately, perhaps with mashed potatoes and a green vegetable.

Pork Meatballs With Bean Stew

Family Favorite

This warming supper dish uses ground pork and chorizo sausage, which you should find in delis. If you can't buy chorizos easily, use a pack of good-quality pork link sausages and peel away the skins

Ingredients for 2

3oz chorizo sausage, rind removed
¾ cup lean ground pork
1 small onion, chopped
1 tsp cumin seeds
salt
black pepper, freshly ground
1 tbsp all-purpose flour
1 tbsp olive oil
1 small red onion, sliced
½ yellow bell pepper, sliced
14oz can cannellini or lima beans, drained
1¼ cups chicken stock
1 sprig fresh rosemary
½ tsp balsamic vinegar

Ingredients for 4

6oz chorizo sausage, rind removed
1¾ cups lean pork mince
1 medium onion, chopped
2 tsp cumin seeds
salt
black pepper, freshly ground
2 tbsp all-purpose flour
2 tbsp olive oil
1 large red onion, sliced
1 yellow bell pepper, sliced
2 x 14oz cans cannellini or lima beans, drained
2½ cups chicken stock
2 sprigs fresh rosemary
1 tsp balsamic vinegar

15 minutes preparation
25 minutes cooking

1 Put the chorizo sausage and ground pork in a food processor with the onion and cumin seeds and season with salt and black pepper. Process until mixed to a coarse paste.

2 Divide into 8 (16) pieces, roll into balls then coat each ball in plain flour. Heat half the oil in a nonstick skillet and fry the meatballs over a medium heat for 4 minutes until browned all over.

3 Remove the meatballs from the skillet with a slotted spoon. Heat the remaining oil and add the onions and pepper, and cook until browned and softened.

4 Add the beans, stock, rosemary, and vinegar and bring to a boil. Return the meatballs to the pan and simmer for 15 minutes. Season and serve.

Sizzling Sausage Bake

Family Favorite

This is such an easy supper dish to rustle up after a busy day. Just throw all the ingredients in a roasting pan and put your feet up.

10 minutes preparation
25 minutes cooking

Ingredients for 2

1lb small new potatoes, quartered
1 clove garlic, crushed
1 tbsp sunflower oil
sea salt
8 pork cocktail wiener
8oz cherry tomatoes
1 tbsp green pesto

Ingredients for 4

2lb small new potatoes, quartered
2 cloves garlic, crushed
2 tbsp sunflower oil
sea salt
16 pork cocktail wiener
1lb cherry tomatoes
2 tbsp green pesto

10 minutes preparation
25 minutes cooking

1 Preheat the oven to 400°F. Put the potatoes in a large roasting pan with the garlic and oil. Season with sea salt, toss the potato wedges, then bake for 10 minutes.

2 Prick the sausages all over with a fork, add to the pan, and toss in the oil. Bake for 10 minutes.

3 Add the tomatoes, toss in the pesto and bake for a

further 5–10 minutes until the tomatoes and sausages are tender and cooked.

4 Divide between warmed plates and serve with green beans.

Home-made Burgers

Freezer Friendly

Make a batch of these burgers for your freezer. You'll know they don't contain chemical additives or colorings, and they taste so much better than bought ones

10 minutes preparation
8 minutes cooking

Ingredients for 2

1½ cups very lean, ground beef
1 small onion, finely chopped
½ egg, beaten
1 tbsp fresh breadcrumbs
1 tsp Worcestershire sauce
¼ tsp dried red pepper flakes
½ tsp mustard
salt
black pepper, freshly ground
2 tsp sunflower oil

To serve

2 ciabatta rolls
2 romaine lettuce leaves
1 beefstake tomato, sliced
2 tsp mayonnaise

Ingredients for 4

3 cups very lean, ground beef
1 medium-sized onion, finely chopped
1 egg, beaten
1¾ tbsp fresh breadcrumbs
2 tsp Worcestershire sauce
½ tsp dried red pepper flakes
1 tsp mustard
salt
black pepper, freshly ground
4 tsp sunflower oil

To serve

4 ciabatta rolls
4 romaine lettuce leaves
2 beefstake tomatoes, sliced
4 tsp mayonnaise

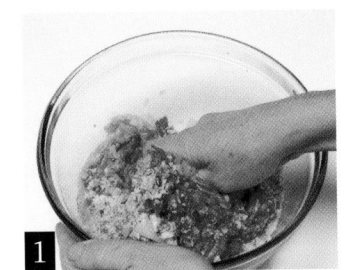

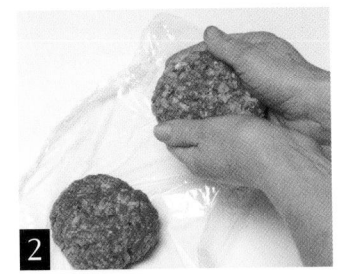

1 Put the ground beef, onion, egg, breadcrumbs, and seasonings in a bowl and season with salt and pepper. Mix together with your hands until thoroughly combined.

2 Divide the mixture into 2 (4) patties. Wrap each one with plastic wrap and freeze for 5 minutes until firm.

3 Heat the oil in a nonstick skillet and fry the burgers for 4 minutes on each side until browned.

4 Meanwhile, cut the rolls in half and toast them lightly. Fill each roll with a lettuce leaf and tomato slices, then top each with a teaspoon of mayonnaise. Add the hot beef burgers and serve immediately.

Smoked Haddock & Potato Wedges

Family Favorite

Frozen fish fillets are a great standby for your freezer. Add just a few fresh ingredients to enjoy this tasty supper dish.

15 minutes preparation
12-14 minutes cooking

Ingredients for 2

8oz potatoes, peeled
1 small zucchini
6oz smoked haddock fillet, skinned and roughly chopped
1 green onion, finely chopped
1 tbsp sunflower oil
2 eggs, beaten
$1/3$ cup light cream or evaporated milk
salt and white pepper
1¾ tbsp Edam cheese, grated

Ingredients for 4

1lb potatoes, peeled
1 large zucchini
12oz smoked haddock fillet, skinned and roughly chopped
2 green onions, finely chopped
2 tbsp sunflower oil
4 eggs, beaten
¾ cup light cream or evaporated milk
salt and white pepper
¼ cup Edam cheese, grated

1 Boil the potatoes in a pan of salted water for 10 minutes to half-cook them. Drain and cool.

2 Coarsely grate the potatoes and the zucchini into a bowl and stir in the haddock and green onions. Heat the oil in a nonstick skillet and fry the mixture for 4 minutes, stirring, until the mixture begins to turn golden.

3 Beat the eggs with the cream or milk and seasoning. Pour over the browned mixture, stir, and shake the skillet. Cook, without stirring until the egg mixture begins to set, which should be for about 4 minutes.

4 Meanwhile, preheat a broiler to hot. Sprinkle the grated cheese over the top of the skillet and place it under the broiler for 3 minutes until the topping is golden. Then serve cut into wedges with a green-leaf salad and chunks of crusty bread.

Thai Chicken Curry

Quick and Easy

Expensive ready-meals seem to take ages to heat through and cost a fortune. Try this quick-cook Thai dish at home for a fraction of the cost

Ingredients for 2

- **2 tsp sunflower oil**
- **12oz skinless, boneless chicken breasts, diced**
- **1 tbsp Thai red-curry paste**
- **1¾ tbsp coconut-milk powder**
- **6 tbsp evaporated milk, mixed with 6 tbsp water**
- **1 small stick lemongrass, chopped**
- **½ tsp Thai fish sauce**
- **1 kaffir lime leaf (optional)**
- **2 tbsp fresh cilantro leaves, chopped**

Ingredients for 4

- **1 tbsp sunflower oil**
- **1½lb skinless, boneless chicken breasts, diced**
- **2 tbsp Thai red-curry paste**
- **¼ cup coconut-milk powder**
- **14oz can evaporated milk, mixed with ½ cup water**
- **1 stick lemon grass, chopped**
- **1 tsp Thai fish sauce**
- **2 kaffir lime leaves (optional)**
- **4 tbsp fresh cilantro leaves, chopped**

10 minutes preparation

15 minutes cooking

1 Heat the oil in a large skillet and lightly brown the chicken pieces. Add the red-curry paste and stir to coat the chicken.

2 Mix the coconut-milk powder in a pitcher with the evaporated milk and water.

3 Add to the skillet with the chopped lemongrass, fish sauce, and lime leaf or leaves and bring to the boil.

4 Lower the heat and simmer for 10–15 minutes, stirring frequently, until the chicken is tender. Just before serving, fold in the fresh cilantro. Serve with boiled rice or rice noodles.

Oven-baked Fish & Fries

Family Favorite

If you run out of frozen oven fries – don't panic. Make your own delicious version—they're much cheaper and they have the same cooking time, too!

Ingredients for 2

1lb 2oz russet potatoes
2 tbsp sunflower oil
2 tbsp all-purpose flour
2 x 6oz cod fillets,
    skinned
2 tbsp mayonnaise
4 small gherkins, sliced

Ingredients for 4

2lb 4 oz russet potatoes
4 tbsp sunflower oil
4 tbsp all-purpose flour
4 x 6oz cod fillets,
    skinned
4 tbsp mayonnaise
8 small gherkins, sliced

10 minutes preparation
25 minutes cooking

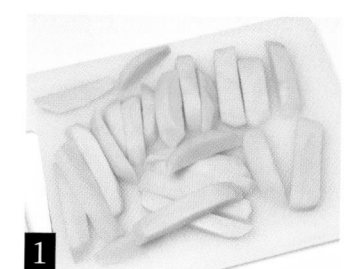

1 Preheat the oven to 425°F. Scrub and peel the potatoes and cut into 1in-thick slices, then cut each slice into thick fries.

2 Place the fries in a pan of boiling water and boil for 3 minutes. Drain well and spread out on paper towels to remove all the water.

3 Place the fries in a bowl and toss in half of the oil to coat. Bake in a roasting pan for 25 minutes, turning over once with a slotted spatula.

4 Sixteen minutes before the fries are baked, heat the remaining oil in a large nonstick skillet. Dust the fish all over with flour, then cook on one side for 4 minutes. Turn the fish over and cook for another 4 minutes. Place on a roasting pan in the oven on a shelf under the fries to finish cooking for 6 minutes. Serve with mayonnaise and sliced gherkins.

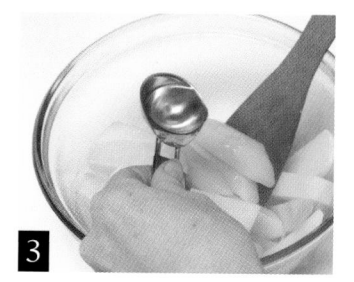

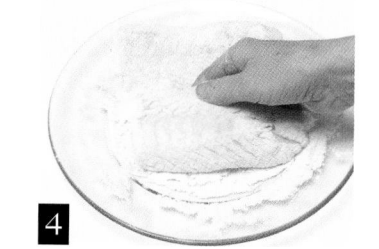

Skillet Stew

Family Favorite

You won't need exotic ingredients for this hearty dish and it cheers everyone up on a cold winter's evening.

Ingredients for 2

- 1lb potatoes
- 4 tsp sunflower oil
- 1 medium-sized onion, thinly sliced into rings
- 4 herby pork link sausages
- 4oz white mushrooms, quartered
- ½ cup beef stock
- 2 tbsp tomato paste
- 1 tsp Worcestershire sauce

Ingredients for 4

- 2lb potatoes
- 2 tbsp sunflower oil
- 2 medium-sized onions, thinly sliced into rings
- 8 herby pork link sausages
- 8oz white mushrooms, quartered
- 1¼ cups beef stock
- 4 tbsp tomato paste
- 2 tsp Worcestershire sauce

10 minutes preparation
25 minutes cooking

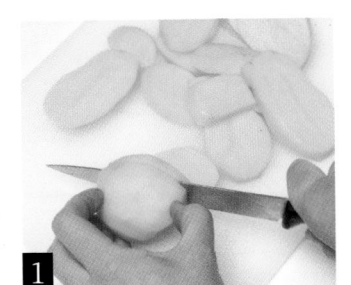

1 Peel the potatoes and cut into thick slices. Place in a pan of boiling water and cook for 5 minutes until just soft. Drain.

2 Meanwhile, heat half of the oil in a large skillet and fry the onions for 2 minutes to soften. Add the sausages and mushrooms and fry for 8 minutes until browned all over.

3 Add the stock, tomato and Worcestershire sauces and cook over a medium heat for 5 minutes until the liquid begins to thicken.

4 Heat the broiler to hot. Toss the potatoes in the remaining oil and spread in a layer over the top of the skillet. Broil for 5–8 minutes until the top of the potatoes are browned and crisp.

Cook's Tip:

To save time, use 1 (for 2 people) or 2 (for 4) 14oz package or packages of ready-sliced and cooked, long-life potatoes (these are sold in your local supermarket).

Italian Meatball & Pasta Bake

Quick and Easy

Soft, fresh pasta really does take just minutes to cook, making this dish superquick. If you can't buy fresh pasta, don't worry, use dried instead.

Ingredients for 2

- 7oz good-quality pork link sausages
- 1 tbsp sunflower oil
- 5oz package fresh trompetti pasta
- 10½oz jar tomato and chile sauce
- 2 tbsp mascarpone cheese
- 1½ tbsp Cheddar cheese, grated
- 1¾ tbsp breadcrumbs

Ingredients for 4

- 14oz good-quality pork link sausages
- 2 tbsp sunflower oil
- 9oz package fresh trompetti pasta
- 2 x 10½oz jars tomato and chile sauce
- 4 tbsp mascarpone cheese
- ¼ cup Cheddar cheese, grated
- ¼ cup breadcrumbs

15 minutes preparation

15 minutes cooking

1 Preheat the oven to 375°F. Put a large pan of lightly salted water on to boil. Now snip the skin away from the sausages with a pair of kitchen scissors.

2 Divide each sausage into three and roll into balls. Heat the oil in a skillet and fry over a medium heat for 8 minutes until golden and evenly browned. Place in a large ovenproof dish.

3 Meanwhile cook the pasta, according to the package instructions until *al dente* and then drain well. Place in the dish with the meatballs. Heat the tomato sauce and mix with the mascarpone, then mix into the dish.

4 Scatter over the cheese and breadcrumbs and bake for 15 minutes until the top is golden and bubbling.

Ham, Cheese & Fish Broils

Quick and Easy

If your children hate fish, try this recipe out on them. They will love the crispy topping on these quick broils.

Ingredients for 2

1 tbsp butter, melted
2 chunky cod or haddock
  steaks 4oz each
2 slices paper-thin ham
1¾ tbsp Cheddar cheese,
  grated

Ingredients for 4

1¾ tbsp butter, melted
4 chunky cod or haddock
  steaks 4oz each
4 slices paper-thin ham
¼ cup Cheddar cheese,
  grated

5 minutes preparation
8 minutes cooking

1 Preheat the boiler to high. Brush a large, shallow, ovenproof dish with butter, place the fish steaks in the dish and brush them with the remaining butter.

2 Broil the fish for 2 minutes under a high heat. Remove from the heat and turn each fish steak over with a slotted spatula. Top each steak with a slice of scrunched ham.

3 Scatter the cheese over the ham and return to the broiler. Cook for 5 minutes.

4 Test the fish with the point of a knife. When the fish flakes easily, it is cooked. Serve immediately, perhaps with broccoli and boiled new potatoes.

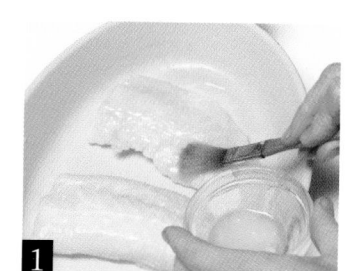

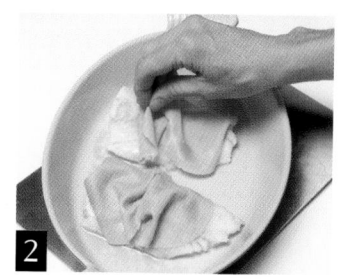

Chili with Red Kidney Beans

Freezer-friendly

This spicy supper dish can be easily made well ahead of time, or frozen, as it reheats really well.

8 minutes preparation

20 minutes cooking

Ingredients for 2

2 tsp sunflower oil
1 cup lean ground sirloin
½ bunch green onions, sliced
1 green jalapeno pepper, deseeded and chopped
1 small red bell pepper, deseeded and finely sliced
½ tsp red chili powder
½ tsp cumin seeds
7oz can diced tomatoes in their juice
7oz can red kidney beans, drained
1 tbsp A1 steak sauce
1 tbsp fresh cilantro, chopped

Ingredients for 4

1 tbsp sunflower oil
2 cups lean ground sirloin
1 bunch green onions, finely sliced
2 green jalapeno peppers, deseeded and chopped
1 red bell pepper, deseeded and finely sliced
1 tsp red chili powder
1 tsp cumin seeds
14oz can diced tomatoes in their juice
14oz can red kidney beans, drained
2 tbsp A1 steak sauce
2 tbsp fresh cilantro, chopped

1 Heat a large skillet or wok, then heat the oil in it and fry the ground sirloin for 5 minutes, until browned.

2 Add the green onions, jalapeno. and bell pepper and fry for 3 minutes to soften.

3 Stir in the spices and cook for a minute. Add the tomatoes, 3 (6) tablespoons of water and cook for 5 minutes.

4 Add the beans and sauce and cook for a further 5 minutes until thickened and bubbling. Serve sprinkled with chopped cilantro and on plain boiled rice.

Curried Chicken, Rice, & Peas

Quick and Easy

Enjoy this quick and tasty way to use up leftover cooked chicken or turkey.

Ingredients for 2

- **2 tsp sunflower oil**
- **½ red chile pepper, deseeded and chopped**
- **1 small onion, finely chopped**
- **2oz white mushrooms, sliced**
- **1 tbsp medium-strength curry paste**
- **1 cup frozen rice**
- **½ cup frozen peas**
- **8oz cooked chicken, skinned and diced**
- **¼ cup cashew nuts**

Ingredients for 4

- **4 tsp sunflower oil**
- **1 red chile pepper, deseeded and chopped**
- **1 medium-sized onion, finely chopped**
- **4oz white mushrooms, sliced**
- **2 tbsp medium-strength curry paste**
- **2 cups frozen rice**
- **1 cup frozen peas**
- **1lb cooked chicken, skinned and diced**
- **½ cup cashew nuts**

10 minutes preparation

10 minutes cooking

1 Heat the oil in a large skillet or wok and fry the chile pepper, onion, and mushrooms for 4 minutes until tender.

2 Add the curry paste and stir together for 1 minute. Add the frozen rice and peas and stir together, adding a little water if necessary.

3 Stir-fry for 4 minutes, until the rice and peas are cooked through and piping hot.

4 Add the chicken and nuts and stir together over a medium heat for 2–3 minutes. Then serve.

Chicken Sticks

No Fat

This is a baked version of those crispy chicken nuggets that kids love. It is much healthier because these sticks are not fried and are not greasy.

Ingredients for 2

9oz skinless, boneless
**   chicken breasts**
1 tbsp all-purpose flour
salt
white pepper
1 small egg
¼ cup dried breadcrumbs
1 tbsp sesame seeds

Ingredients for 4

1lb 2oz skinless,
**   boneless chicken breasts**
1¾ tbsps all-purpose flour
ssalt
white pepper
1 large egg
½ cup dried breadcrumbs
2 tbsp sesame seeds

15 minutes preparation

15 minutes cooking

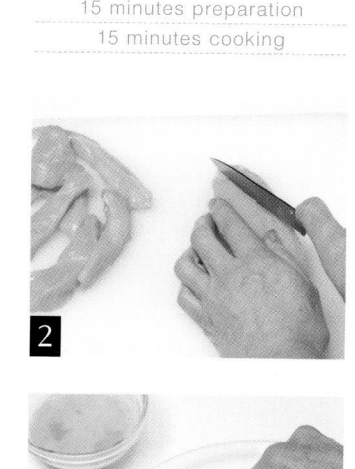

1 Preheat the oven to 400°F. Grease two cookie sheets or a large roasting pan.

2 Cut the chicken into strips. Place the flour on a plate and season with salt and white pepper. Beat the egg and place in a separate bowl. Mix the breadcrumbs and sesame seeds together and place on another plate.

3 Roll the chicken strips in the flour, dip into the egg, and then roll in the breadcrumb mixture.

4 Place on the cookie sheets and bake for 10–15 minutes until golden. Serve with fries and salad.

Cook's Tip:

To make a dipping sauce to serve with the chicken, blend 4 tbsp peanut butter with 1 tbsp honey, 3 tbsp water, 2 tsp soy sauce and 1 tsp tomato ketchup in a small pan. Heat gently, then transfer the sauce to a bowl and serve.

Crunchy Cod Pie

Family Favorite

With a stock of frozen fish fillets in your freezer, you can always rustle up a healthy meal.

Ingredients for 2

2 x 3½oz frozen cod
  fillets
1 tbsp butter
1 small onion, finely
  chopped
2 stalks celery, finely sliced
4oz broccoli florets
1 tbsp all-purpose flour
½ cup milk
¼ cup grated cheese
salt
black pepper, freshly ground
1 x 1oz pack plain potato
  chips

Ingredients for 4

4 x 3½oz frozen cod
  fillets
1¾ tbsp butter
1 medium-sized onion, finely
  chopped
4 stalks celery, finely sliced
8oz broccoli florets
2 tbsp all-purpose flour
1¼ cups milk
½ cup grated cheese
salt
black pepper, freshly ground
2 x 1oz packs plain potato
  chips

10 minutes preparation
10 minutes cooking

1 Preheat the oven to 350°F. Grease a heatproof dish. Now cut the frozen fish into 1in cubes.

2 Heat the butter in a large skillet and fry the onion and celery for 4 minutes to soften. Add the broccoli florets and fry for 3 minutes. Stir in the flour and cook for 1 minute.

3 Gradually add the milk and cook for 1–2 minutes until thickened. Stir in the cod and half of the grated cheese and then season with salt and black pepper.

4 Pour into the dish, crush the hips, and scatter over the top with the remaining cheese and bake for 15–20 minutes until golden.

Pork Chops With Lima-bean Mash

Family Favorite

Canned beans are a really healthy option and with no soaking and little cooking, they are a very quick choice for supper

10 minutes preparation

12 minutes cooking

Ingredients for 2

1 x 14oz can lima beans
finely grated zest and juice
   of ¼ lemon
2 thick pork-loin chops
salt
Black pepper, freshly ground
1 tbsp butter
1 sprig fresh thyme or ½
   tsp dried thyme
¾ cup dry cider
2 tbsp heavy cream

Ingredients for 4

2 x 14oz cans lima beans
Finely grated zest and juice
   of ½ lemon
4 thick pork-loin chops
salt
black pepper, freshly ground
1¾ tbsps butter
2 sprigs fresh thyme or 1 tsp
   dried thyme
1½ cups dry cider
4 tbsp heavy cream

1 Drain the beans and place in a saucepan with ½ cup (1¼ cups) water. Bring to the boil, then simmer for 10 minutes until the beans are soft and separating. Press through a sieve, add the lemon zest and juice and return to the rinsed-out pan, then warm up just before serving.

2 Trim the chops of any extra fat and season on both sides with salt and freshly ground black pepper.

3 Melt the butter in a nonstick skillet and fry the chops with the thyme for about 6 minutes on each side.

4 When the chops are cooked, keep them warm on serving plates. Pour in the cider and let it bubble until it reduces by half, then stir in the cream. Serve with the chops, sauce, mashed beans, and perhaps a green vegetable such as broccoli.

Jacket Potatoes With Frankfurters & Mustard Sauce

Family Favorite

Jacket potatoes baked in the oven are tasty, but cooked in minutes in your microwave oven, they are just as good.

10 minutes preparation

24 minutes cooking

Ingredients for 2

2 large russet potatoes
salt
6oz package frankfurters
1 tsp sunflower oil, plus a
    little extra
2 green onions
1 tbsp whole-grain mustard
7oz can diced tomatoes
1¾ tbsp Edam cheese,
    grated

Ingredients for 4

4 large russet potatoes
salt
12oz package frankfurters
2 tsp sunflower oil, plus a
    little extra
4 green onions
2 tbsp whole-grain mustard
14oz can diced tomatoes
¼ cup Edam cheese,
    grated

1 Scrub the potatoes, dry them and prick them all over with a fork. Rub each potato lightly with a little oil and salt. Place the potatoes on a paper towel and cook in the microwave oven for about 5-6 minutes per potato. Test by squeezing the hot potatoes: if they are soft, then they are ready.

2 Meanwhile, cut the frankfurters into 1in chunks and slice the green onions thinly. Heat the oil in a nonstick skillet and fry the onions and frankfurters for 2 minutes, stirring.

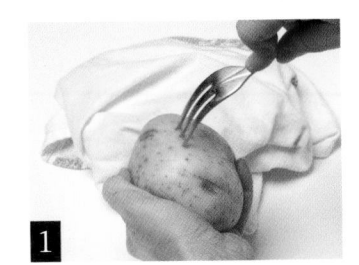

3 Mix in the mustard and tomatoes and simmer for about 5 minutes, stirring occasionally.

4 Cut a cross on top of each potato and split them open. Divide the filling between the hot potatoes, then serve topped with grated cheese.

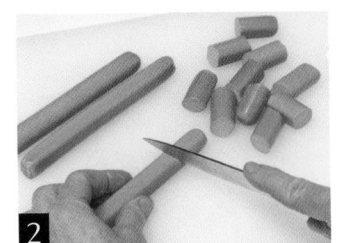

Speedy Spaghetti Bolognese

Quick and Easy

Look for fast-cook pasta or fresh pasta, which takes only minutes to cook. You'll find that mincing vegetables finely in a processor will save on time, too!

10 minutes preparation

15 minutes cooking

Ingredients for 2

2 tsp olive oil
1 cup lean ground beef
1 small onion
2oz white mushrooms
2 tbsp tomato paste
1 tsp dried oregano
½ cup chicken stock
1 tsp cornstarch
6oz quick-cook spaghetti

Ingredients for 4

4 tsp olive oil
2 cups lean ground beef
1 medium-sized onion
4oz white mushrooms
4 tbsp tomato paste
1 tsp dried oregano
1¼ cups chicken stock
2 tsp cornstarch
12oz quick-cook spaghetti

1 Heat the oil in a large, deep saucepan and fry the ground beef for 8 minutes until browned.

2 Chop the onions finely and thenslice the white mushrooms thinly.

3 Add to the pan with the tomato paste, oregano, and stock and cook over a medium heat for 15 minutes. Blend the cornstarch with 1 tablespoon of water and add to the pan. Stir until thickened.

4 Meanwhile, cook the spaghetti according to the package instructions in a large pan of boiling, salted water. Drain and divide between warmed serving bowls. Serve topped with the sauce.

Florentine Pasta

Quick and Easy

Put this tasty supper dish together from the fridge, freezer, and pantry.

Ingredients for 2

2 tsp sunflower oil
¼ cup smoked-bacon lard
leaves or chopped bacon
1 small onion, chopped
6oz rigatoni, penne, or
macaroni pasta
1 cup tomato passata sauce
½ cup frozen, chopped
spinach, thawed
½ cup ricotta cheese
¼ cup mozzarella cheese,
grated
¼ cup Cheddar cheese,
grated

Ingredients for 4

1 tbsp sunflower oil
½ cup smoked-bacon lard
leaves or chopped bacon
1 large onion, chopped
12oz rigatoni, penne, or
macaroni pasta
2 cups tomato passata auce
1 cup frozen, chopped
spinach, thawed
1 cup ricotta cheese
½ cup mozzarella cheese,
grated
½ cup Cheddar cheese
grated

15 minutes preparation
12 minutes cooking

1 Heat the oil in a skillet, add the bacon and onions and fry for 10 minutes, until the fat runs from the bacon and the onions soften.

2 Meanwhile, cook the pasta in a large pan of boiling, salted water according to the package instructions. Drain and return to the pan. Heat the tomato passata in a pan, add half to the pasta, and toss well.

3 Press the water from the spinach through a sieve. Add the spinach and ricotta to the pan, along with the bacon and onions.

4 Toss the spinach mixture into the pasta, add the mozzarella, and then serve, drizzled with the remaining passata, sprinkled with Cheddar cheese.

Quick Tandoori Chicken

spicy

This is an ideal quick meal to serve out of doors on a warm summer's evening. Just pop the roasting pan in the oven and concentrate on making a colorful salad.

Ingredients for 2

4 boneless chicken thighs
juice of ½ small lemon
1 clove garlic, peeled
1in-piece fresh ginger root,
**   peeled**
¼ tsp ground red chile
¼ tsp ground cumin
⅓ cup plain yogurt
½ tsp garam masala
2 tsp ground paprika
2 tsp tomato paste
2 tsp sunflower oil
salt

Ingredients for 4

8 boneless chicken thighs
Juice of 1 small lemon
2 cloves garlic, peeled
2in piece fresh ginger root,
**   peeled**
½ tsp ground red chile
½ tsp ground cumin
½ cup plain yogurt
1 tsp garam masala
1 tbsp ground paprika
1 tbsp tomato paste
1 tbsp sunflower oil
salt

10 minutes preparation
20 minutes cooking

1 Preheat the oven to 400°F. Slash into the skin and flesh of the chicken all over and toss in the lemon juice.

2 Place all the remaining ingredients in a food processor or small blender, add salt to season, and blend until smooth.

3 Toss the chicken in the paste to coat. Place in a large roasting tin and bake for about 20 minutes until tender.

4 Serve piping hot with lemon and tomato wedges and a leafy green salad. Accompany with sliced, warmed naan breads and a chopped cucumber and yogurt raita dish.

Cook's Tip:

If you want to prepare this dish ahead of time, leave the chicken pieces to marinate in the spicy paste in a sealed container in the fridge for 12-24 hours.

Light
Meals

Spaghetti With Cherry Tomatoes

Easy Entertaining

Bocconcini are tiny balls of buffalo-milk mozzarella. They are handy to keep in the fridge for serving on pasta and pizzas.

Ingredients for 2

8oz cherry tomatoes
¼ tsp dried red pepper flakes
1 clove garlic, chopped
½ tsp dried oregano
1 tbsp olive oil
6oz spaghetti
2 tbsp capers in brine, drained
4¼oz Bocconcini buffalo-milk mozzarella balls or diced mozzarella
fresh basil leaves for garnishing

Ingredients for 4

1lb 2oz cherry tomatoes
½ tsp dried red pepper flakes
2 cloves garlic, chopped
1 tsp dried oregano
2 tbsp olive oil
12oz spaghetti
4 tbsp capers in brine, drained
9oz Bocconcini buffalo-milk mozzarella balls or diced mozzarella
fresh basil leaves for garnishing

5 minutes preparation
20 minutes cooking

1 Preheat the oven to 400°F. Place the tomatoes in a non-stick roasting tray with the red pepper flakes, garlic, herbs, and oil and toss together. Bake for 15–20 minutes until the tomatoes have browned and have started to burst open.

2 Meanwhile, cook the spaghetti in a large pan of boiling water, according to the package instructions, until it is *al dente*.

3 Drain the spaghetti well and return to the pan. Add the capers and mozzarella and toss together. Spoon the tomatoes and their juices into the pan.

4 Toss together with two forks. Divide between warmed serving dishes and serve immediately, scattered with fresh basil leaves.

Luxurious Scrambled Eggs

Quick and Easy

This makes the ideal meal for a weekend brunch if you have guests, or a quick, light supper. Look out for packs of smoked-salmon scraps or ask your fish supplier for them, as they are very economical.

Ingredients for 2

2 bagels, sliced in half
4 eggs
salt
black pepper
1 tbsp unsalted butter,
    plus a little extra for
    buttering
1 tbsp heavy cream
1¾ tbsp Parmesan cheese,
    thinly sliced
1 tsp fresh dill, chopped
2oz smoked-salmon
    trimmings

Ingredients for 4

4 bagels, sliced in half
8 eggs
salt
black pepper
1¾ tbsp unsalted butter,
    plus a little extra for
    buttering
2 tbsp heavy cream
¼ cup Parmesan cheese,
    thinly sliced
2 tsp fresh dill, chopped
4oz smoked-salmon
    trimmings

5 minutes preparation
4 minutes cooking

1 Toast the bagels lightly on both sides, butter them lightly and keep them warm on serving plates.

2 Break the eggs into a bowl and season with salt and black pepper. Beat lightly together with a fork until frothy.

3 Heat the butter in a heavy-based saucepan. Pour in the beaten eggs and scramble over a medium heat for about 2 minutes. Stir with a wooden spoon, bringing the outside edges into the middle to stop the eggs sticking.

4 While the eggs are still soft, creamy, and slightly runny, add the cream, cheese, and dill and stir gently for 1 minute. If the smoked salmon is uneven, cut into strips with a pair of kitchen scissors. Fold into the egg mixture and serve immediately.

Mango & Chicken Salad

Low Fat

Make a plain chicken salad into a feast by adding juicy, fresh mango slices

Ingredients for 2

1 large, ripe mango
2 ready-cooked, charbroiled
    chicken breasts
3oz mixed salad leaves
3 tbsp olive oil
1 tbsp fresh lime juice
1 tsp soy sauce
½ small, red chile pepper
2 tbsp fresh cilantro,
chopped

Ingredients for 4

2 small ripe, mangoes
4 ready-cooked, chargrilled
    chicken breasts
5oz mixed salad leaves
6 tbsp olive oil
2 tbsp fresh lime juice
2 tsp soy sauce
1 small, red chile pepper
4 tbsp fresh cilantro,
chopped

10 minutes preparation

No cooking

1 Peel the mango or mangoes with a vegetable peeler or sharp knife, place on a chopping board, and slice two thick sections of flesh away from either side of the central flat stone. Cut away as much of the remaining flesh from the stone as possible, then thinly slice all of the flesh.

2 Slice the chicken diagonally into thin strips and place in a bowl with the mango slices.

3 Divide the salad leaves between the serving plates. Mix the oil, lime juice, and soy sauce together. Deseed and finely chop the chile pepper, being careful not to touch your face as the fiery juice will sting.

4 Add the chile pepper and cilantro to the dressing and whisk together. Pour over the chicken and mangoes, toss well, then serve over the salad leaves.

Salade Niçoise

Easy Entertaining

Although Salade Niçoise has so many delicious flavors, it's simple to make, and you'll find most of the ingredients readily to hand.

Ingredients for 2

5oz small, new potatoes
3 tbsp olive oil
1 tbsp lemon juice
2 eggs
2oz green beans,
   trimmed and halved
3 ripe tomatoes
2 butter lettuces
4oz tuna in oil
1 tbsp capers in brine
¼cup black olives, pitted
4 anchovy fillets

Ingredients for 4

10oz small, new potatoes
5 tbsp olive oil
2 tbsp lemon juice
4 eggs
4oz green beans,
   trimmed and halved
6 ripe tomatoes
4 butter lettuces
8oz can tuna in oil
2 tbsp capers in brine
½ cup black olives, pitted
8 anchovy fillets

15 minutes preparation
15 minutes cooking

1

1 Cook the new potatoes in boiling, salted water until tender (about 12 minutes). Mix the olive oil with the lemon juice to make a dressing. Cut the potatoes in half or quarters, according to size and toss in 1 tablespoon of the dressing while still warm.

2 Bring a pan of water to a rolling boil, add the eggs, and cook for 6 minutes exactly. Drain and immediately plunge into cold water, then peel the eggs before they cool totally. When cold, cut into quarters.

3 Cook the beans in boiling, salted water until tender, drain, and plunge into cold water. Cut the tomatoes into quarters and toss in the dressing with the potato, lettuce, beans, tuna, capers, and olives.

4 Place on serving plates and top with the anchovies and quartered eggs. Serve the salad immediately.

2

3

Chicken With Penne

Easy Entertaining

Combine these tasty Italian ingredients for a special lunch treat.

Ingredients for 2

- **2 chicken breasts**
- **1 tsp olive oil**
- **¼ cup chorizo sausage, peeled and diced**
- **1 small onion, chopped**
- **¼ cup white mushrooms, sliced**
- **7oz can diced tomatoes in their juice**
- **⅓ cup chicken stock**
- **½ tsp dried oregano**
- **¼ cup black olives, pitted**
- **6oz penne pasta**

Ingredients for 4

- **4 chicken breasts**
- **2 tsp olive oil**
- **½ cup chorizo sausage, peeled and diced**
- **1 medium-sized onion, chopped**
- **½ cup white mushrooms, sliced**
- **14oz can diced tomatoes in their juice**
- **¾ cup chicken stock**
- **1 tsp dried oregano**
- **½ cup black olives, pitted**
- **12oz penne pasta**

10 minutes preparation
20 minutes cooking

1 Remove any skin and bones from the chicken breasts and cut the meat into large chunks. Heat the oil in a nonstick skillet and fry the chorizo until the fat runs, for about 2 minutes. Remove with a slotted spoon.

2 Add the chicken, onions, and mushrooms and cook for 5 minutes until browned all over. Add the tomatoes, stock, and herbs and simmer for 5 minutes.

3 Add the olives and chorizo and simmer for a further 5 minutes until the chicken is cooked and the sauce has thickened.

4 Meanwhile, cook the penne according to the package instructions until *al dente*. Drain, divide between warmed serving bowls and top with the sauce before serving.

Oven-baked Tuna Risotto

From the Pantry

Put all of the ingredients into one dish and pop it into the oven—it couldn't be easier!

10 minutes preparation
25 minutes cooking

Ingredients for 2

- 1 tbsp olive oil
- 1 small onion, finely chopped
- ½ cup risotto rice
- ¾ cup oz vegetable stock
- 7oz can diced tomatoes
- 6½oz can tuna in oil, drained
- 2 zucchini, coarsely grated
- salt
- black pepper, freshly ground
- ½ tsp dried oregano
- 1¾ tbsp Parmesan cheese, shaved into curls
- 1 tbsp fresh Italian parsley, chopped

Ingredients for 4

- 2 tbsp olive oil
- 1 large onion, finely chopped
- ¾ cup risotto rice
- 1½ cups vegetable stock
- 14oz can diced tomatoes
- 6½oz cans tuna in oil, drained
- 4 zucchini, coarsely grated
- salt
- black pepper, freshly ground
- 1 tsp dried oregano
- ¼ cup Parmesan cheese, shaved into curls
- 2 tbsp fresh Italian parsley, chopped

1. Preheat the oven to 400°F. Heat the olive oil in a large skillet, add the onion, and cook until soft.

2. Add the rice, stock, and tomatoes and bring to a simmer. Stir in the tuna and zucchini and season with salt, freshly ground black pepper, and herbs. Transfer to a heatproof casserole dish.

3. Put on the lid or cover the casserole dish tightly with a sheet of aluminum foil and then bake for 25 minutes until the rice is tender.

4. Divide between warmed serving bowls and scatter with curls of Parmesan cheese and fresh parsley.

Tagliatelle with a Creamy Bacon Sauce

From the Pantry

I first made this pasta dish when I didn't have time to go shopping, but it is so tasty, it has now become a favorite.

Ingredients for 2

- 6oz tagliatelle pasta
- 2 tsp olive oil
- 4 slices smoked bacon, rinds removed and chopped
- 1/3 cup frozen peas
- 1/4 cup garlic and herb cream cheese
- 1/2 cup light cream
- salt
- black pepper, freshly ground
- 1/4 cup Parmesan cheese, grated
- 2 tbsp fresh parsley, chopped

Ingredients for 4

- 12oz tagliatelle pasta
- 3 tsp olive oil
- 8 slices smoked bacon, rinds removed and chopped
- 3/4 cup frozen peas
- 1/2 cup garlic and herb cream cheese
- 1 1/4 cups light cream
- salt
- black pepper, freshly ground
- 1/2 cup Parmesan cheese, grated
- 3 tbsp fresh parsley, chopped

10 minutes preparation

12 minutes cooking

1 Cook the pasta in a pan of boiling salted water, according to the package instructions, then drain, return to the pan and toss in 1 teaspoon of olive oil.

2 Meanwhile, heat the remaining oil in a skillet and fry the bacon for 3 minutes until crisp.

3 Add the peas, cream cheese, and cream and stir over a low heat until the cheese has melted, for about 2 minutes. Season with salt and freshly ground black pepper.

4 Add half of the Parmesan cheese and parsley and stir into the cooked pasta in the pan. Toss together using two forks. Serve in warmed bowls and top with the remaining cheese and parsley.

Sautéed Cheese Toasties

Superquick

The sharpness of Lancashire cheese (a hard, firm, English cheese) blends well with spicy relish and the crunch of whole-grain bread. Serve as a snack or with soup.

Ingredients for 2

- 1 tbsp butter, softened
- 4 slices multi-grain, whole-wheat bread
- 2 slices ham
- 2 tbsp spicy brown relish
- 4oz Lancashire or Cheddar cheese, thinly sliced
- 2 tbsp sunflower oil

Ingredients for 4

- 1¾ tbsp butter, softened
- 8 slices multi-grain, whole-wheat bread
- 4 slices ham
- 4 tbsp spicy brown relish
- 8oz Lancashire or Cheddar cheese, thinly sliced
- 4 tbsp sunflower oil

5 minutes preparation

5 minutes cooking

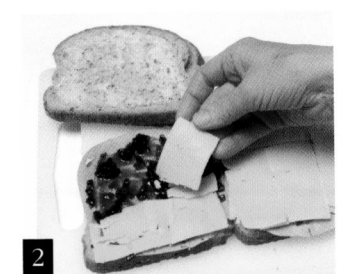

1 Spread the bread lightly on one side with the butter. Place the ham on top.

2 Spoon the relish over the ham and smooth it out. Top with the sliced cheese.

3 Place the remaining bread slice on top. Repeat to make the remaining sandwiches. Heat half the oil in a large nonstick skillet until the skillet is hot. Place the sandwich on the hot skillet and press down with a slotted spatula or small plate.

4 Cook over a high heat for 2 minutes, pressing down constantly. Lift the sandwich out of the skillet with a slotted spatula and turn it over. Heat the remaining oil in the skillet and fry the other side for 2 minutes, pressing down again. Serve immediately. Repeat to make the remaining sandwiches, serving each one when it is piping hot.

Chicken Caesar Salad

Family Favorite

This is one of my favorite quick lunches: succulent chicken, with lots of crisp lettuce and crunchy croutons, all topped with a lively dressing to give it extra bite.

Ingredients for 2

- 3 tbsp lemon juice
- 1 clove garlic, crushed
- 2 tsp French mustard
- 2 skinned, boneless chicken breasts
- salt
- black pepper, freshly ground
- 4 thick slices white bread
- 2 tsp white-wine vinegar
- 1/3 cup plain yogurt
- 1½ tbsp mayonnaise
- ¼ cup Parmesan cheese, shaved into curls
- 1 romaine lettuce

Ingredients for 4

- 6 tbsp lemon juice
- 2 cloves garlic, crushed
- 4 tsp French mustard
- 4 skinned, boneless chicken breasts
- salt
- black pepper, freshly ground
- 8 thick slices white bread
- 4 tsp white-wine vinegar
- ¾ cup plain yoghurt
- 3 tbsp mayonnaise
- ½ cup Parmesan cheese, shaved into curls
- 2 romaine lettuces

15 minutes preparation
10 minutes cooking

1 Preheat the broiler to hot and line the broiler pan with aluminum foil. Mix 2 (4) tablespoons of the lemon juice with the garlic and half of the mustard and smear over the chicken breasts. Season with salt and pepper and broil the chicken on both sides for 10 minutes until tender. Cool.

2 Cut the crusts from the bread and toast lightly on both sides. Cool, then cut into 1in cubes.

3 Put the remaining lemon juice and mustard in a blender or small processor with the vinegar, yogurt, mayonnaise, and half of the Parmesan cheese, and blend until smooth.

4 Slice the cold chicken into strips and toss in half of the dressing. Break the lettuce into leaves, chop into thick slices, and arrange on serving plates with the chicken and croutons. Drizzle over the remaining dressing and Parmesan cheese.

Bacon & Bean Minestrone

Freezer Friendly

You can make this warming soup ahead of time, as the flavors improve on reheating, or make a double batch for the freezer

Ingredients for 2

- 2 tsp olive oil
- 1 small onion, peeled and chopped
- 2oz bacon, rinds removed and diced
- 1 clove garlic, peeled and crushed
- 1 stalk celery, finely chopped
- 1 large carrot, diced
- 2 tbsp tomato paste
- 2½ cups vegetable stock
- 14oz can cannellini beans, rinsed and drained
- ½ small savoy cabbage, finely shredded
- salt
- black pepper, freshly ground

Ingredients for 4

- 1 tbsp olive oil
- 1 large onion, peeled and chopped
- 4oz bacon, rinds removed and diced
- 2 cloves garlic, peeled and crushed
- 2 stalks celery, finely chopped
- 2 carrots, diced
- 4 tbsp tomato paste
- 4¼ cups vegetable stock
- 2 x 14oz cans cannellini beans, rinsed and drained
- 1 small savoy cabbage, finely shredded
- salt
- black pepper, freshly ground

10 minutes preparation

22 minutes cooking

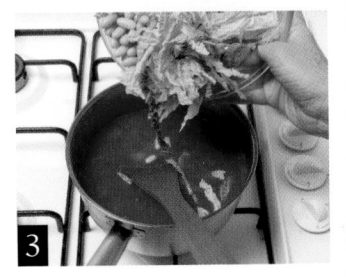

1 Heat the oil in a large pan and fry the onion and bacon until golden, for about 2 minutes.

2 Add the garlic, celery and carrots and fry for 4 minutes then stir in the tomato paste and the stock. Bring to a boil, then cover, and simmer for 10 minutes.

3 Add the beans and the cabbage and simmer for a further 10 minutes, until the cabbage is tender.

4 Taste the soup and season, then serve in warmed bowls with chunks of crusty bread.

Frittata

Easy Entertaining

This omelet-type recipe fills up a medium-sized skillet, so if you want to feed 4, you'll have to make another frittata separately. It makes a delicious summer dish served with lots of green salad leaves.

Ingredients for 2

6 eggs
1 tbsp fresh parsley, chopped
1 tbsp fresh basil, chopped
1 tbsp fresh chives, chopped
salt
black pepper, freshly ground
1 tbsp olive oil
1 onion, sliced into rings
1 zucchini, thinly sliced
1 yellow or orange bell pepper, deseeded and thinly sliced
5oz cherry tomatoes, halved
5oz green olives, pitted and sliced
¼ cup Parmesan cheese, grated

10 minutes preparation
11-12 minutes cooking

1 Place the eggs and the herbs in a measuring pitcher with half an eggshellful of cold water. Season with salt and pepper and whisk together until blended.

2 Heat the oil in a nonstick skillet and fry the onions, zucchini, and pepper for 3 minutes until softened. Add the tomatoes, olives, and half the cheese to the pan.

3 Pour in the egg mixture and stir. Cook over a medium heat for about 5 minutes, until almost firm.

4 Heat the broiler to hot. Sprinkle over the remaining cheese and broil for 3 minutes until the top is firm and golden. Cut into wedges and serve with a salad of mixed green leaves, including watercress.

Cook's Tip:

If you don't have a fresh bell pepper, you could use 4oz roasted peppers from a jar instead, drained of their oil and sliced.

Goat-cheese Bruschettas

Family Favorite

The bright-red, charboiled peppers that come in jars have a wonderful, intense flavor. Try serving luscious, melting goat cheese on crusty, toasted ciabatta bread—it may be straight from the pantry, but this dish has a real Mediterranean twist.

Ingredients for 2

- ⅓ cup charbroiled red peppers, preserved in oil
- ½ loaf ciabatta bread
- 1¾ tbsp butter, softened
- 1 tsp tomato paste
- 1 tbsp fresh basil, chopped
- 1 x 4oz round goat cheese
- 8 black olives, pitted
- black pepper

Ingredients for 4

- ¾ cup charbroiled red peppers, preserved in oil
- 1 loaf ciabatta bread
- ¼ cup butter, softened
- 2 tsp tomato paste
- 2 tbsp fresh basil, chopped
- 2 x 4oz rounds goat cheese
- 16 black olives, pitted
- black pepper

5 minutes preparation
8 minutes cooking

1 Drain the peppers, and slice them, reserving the oil from the jar.

2 Cut the bread in half lengthways then cut into 4 (8) squares. Lightly toast the bread on both sides under a medium-hot broiler until it is just pale.

3 Beat the butter with the tomato paste and the basil and spread thinly on the cut side of the toasted bread.

4 Slice or cut the goat cheese to fit on the bread. Top with sliced peppers, and scatter over the olives. Drizzle each with a little oil from the jar. Cook under a hot broiler for 3–5 minutes until the cheese is melted and bubbling. Serve immediately with plenty of freshly ground black pepper.

Fusilli With Salmon & Garlic Cream

Superquick

This simple combination of pasta and the rich flavor of salmon in a creamy sauce is irresistible

10 minutes preparation
12 minutes cooking

Ingredients for 2

**5oz fusilli or spaghetti
pasta
1 tbsp butter
1 small clove garlic, crushed
¼ tsp grated nutmeg
1¾ tbsp Parmesan cheese,
grated
¼ cup canned red salmon,
drained
2 tbsp fresh parsley,
chopped
5 tbsp heavy cream
salt
black pepper, freshly ground**

Ingredients for 4

**10oz fusilli or spaghetti
pasta
1¾ tbs[butter
1 clove garlic, crushed
¼ tsp grated nutmeg
¼ cup Parmesan cheese,
grated
¾ cup canned red salmon,
drained
4 tbsp fresh parsley,
chopped
2/3 cup heavy cream
salt
black pepper, freshly ground**

1 Cook the pasta in a large pan of boiling, salted water for 8–10 minutes or according to the package instructions, until *al dente*.

2 Drain the pasta, then add the butter, nutmeg, and garlic to the cooking pan and cook for 1 minute. Return the pasta and half the Parmesan to the pan and toss together.

3 Flake the salmon into a bowl and stir together with the parsley and cream.

4 Add to the pan with the hot pasta and toss together with two forks. Season and serve in warmed bowls, sprinkled with the remaining cheese. Accompany with a salad of mixed green leaves.

Smoked Ham, Cheese, & Chive Omelet

Quick and Easy

This delicious dish cuts down on shopping time and dish-washing. It is made from basic ingredients from your fridge and cooked in no time in a single skillet!

5 minutes preparation

5 minutes cooking

Ingredients for 2

3 eggs
salt
white pepper
1 tbsp milk
1 tbsp butter
½ cup smoked ham, diced
½ bunch fresh chives,
    snipped
½ cup Edam cheese,
    grated

Ingredients for 4

6 eggs
salt
white pepper
2 tbsp milk
1¾ tbsp butter
1 cup smoked ham, diced
1 bunch fresh chives,
    snipped
1 cup Edam cheese,
    grated

1 Break the eggs into a bowl and season with salt and white pepper. Now, using a fork, beat together with the milk until smooth.

2 Heat a medium (large) nonstick skillet, add the butter and then swirl to coat the skillet.

3 Pour in the egg mixture and sprinkle over the ham, chives, and half of the grated cheese. Stir gently to mix.

4 Heat the broiler. Cook the omelet over a medium heat for about 2 minutes until the base starts to firm. Sprinkle over the remaining cheese and place the skillet under the hot broiler for 1–2 minutes until the top is set and golden. Serve in wedges with crusty bread, and a salad of crisp green leaves with tomatoes.

French-bread Pizzas

From the Pantry

You'll find that part-baked French bread is very handy—it keeps in the fridge or freezer for some time and can be freshly baked when needed.

Ingredients for 2

1 small, par-baked French
   bread
2 tbsp tomato paste
1 tsp garlic paste
¼ cup mozzarella cheese,
   diced
4 black olives, pitted and
   sliced
1 small, spicy pepperoni
⅓ cup charbroiled red
   peppers in oil, sliced
salt
black pepper, freshly ground
2 tsp olive oil
1 tbsp fresh basil, chopped

Ingredients for 4

2 small, par-baked French
   bread
4 tbsp tomato paste
2 tsp garlic paste
½ cup mozzarella cheese,
   diced
8 black olives, pitted and
   sliced
2 small, spicy pepperoni
¾ cup charbroiled red
   peppers in oil, sliced
salt
black pepper, freshly ground
4 tsp olive oil
2 tbsp fresh basil, chopped

5 minutes preparation
20 minutes cooking

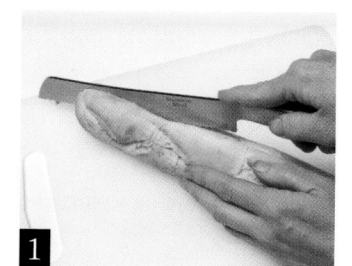

1 Preheat the oven to 400°F. Bake the French bread according to the package instructions, for about 8 minutes. Cool slightly, then cut in half lengthways.

2 Mix the tomato paste and garlic paste together and spread evenly over the 2 (4) pieces of bread.

3 Divide the remaining ingredients, except for the oil and basil, arrange on top of the tomato paste, and then season well.

4 Place on a cookie sheet and drizzle the oil over. Bake for 12 minutes, until the cheese melts. Serve hot, sprinkled with the basil.

Skillet Pizza

Family Favorite

You won't need to turn your oven on to make this tasty pizza. Add all of your favorite toppings, plus plenty of melted cheese.

Ingredients for 2

5oz pack pizza-base mix
2 tbsp sunflower oil
1 large onion, sliced into rings
½ cup mushrooms, sliced
½ cup tomato passata sauce
1 tsp dried oregano
1 tbsp capers in brine, drained
3oz salami slices, halved
6 anchovies in oil, drained and halved
½ cup mozzarella cheese, chopped

10 minutes preparation
18 minutes cooking

1 Make up the pizza base with water following the package instructions, knead well, and roll out to a circle large enough to fit inside a 10in skillet.

2 Heat 1 tablespoon of the oil and cook the onions and mushrooms for 5 minutes, until soft. Remove from the skillet with a slotted spoon.

3 Heat the remaining oil and place the dough in the skillet. Cook over a medium heat for 5 minutes, until the base is lightly browned. Turn the base over and cook for a further 5 minutes.

4 While the other side is cooking, spoon over the passata sauce and herbs. Arrange the cooked onions and mushrooms, on it, then top with the capers, salami, anchovies, and cheese. To serve, place the skillet under a hot broiler and broil for 2 minutes, until the cheese is bubbling. Lift out of the skillet with 2 spatulas and then cut into 4 wedges to serve.

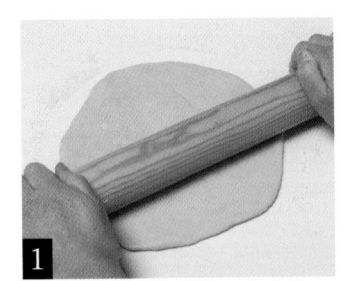

Mushroom & Bacon Kedgeree

Family Favorite

This British delicacy uses bacon instead of the traditional fish, and it makes an ideal brunch dish.

Ingredients for 2

4oz long-grain rice
1 tbsp butter
4 slices smoked Canadian bacon
1 red onion, peeled and chopped
1 small, green bell pepper, deseeded and finely chopped
4oz white mushrooms, quartered
1/3 cup sour cream
1/4 tsp ground cumin
2 tbsp fresh cilantro, chopped

Ingredients for 4

8oz long-grain rice
1¾ tbsp butter
8 slices smoked Canadian bacon
2 red onions, peeled and chopped
1 green bell pepper, deseeded and finely chopped
8oz white mushrooms, quartered
½ cup sour cream
½ tsp ground cumin
4 tbsp fresh cilantro, chopped

10 minutes preparation
20 minutes cooking

1 Rinse the rice in cold water, then add to a large pan of boiling, salted water. Stir the rice, cover, and cook for about 10 minutes, until the rice is just tender.

2 Meanwhile, heat the butter in a large nonstick skillet. Dice the bacon and fry for about 2 minutes, until the fat runs. Remove from the skillet with a slotted spoon.

3 Add the chopped onions and bell pepper and fry for 3 minutes until softened. Add the mushrooms and sauté for 3 minutes to brown,

4 Drain the rice and add to the skillet with the cooked bacon, sour cream, and cumin. Stir over a moderate heat for 3 minutes until warmed through. Serve sprinkled with cilantro.

Lamb Koftas

spicy

Try this Greek-inspired combination of spicy broiled lamb served with warm pita breads, crunchy, mixed-leaf green salad, and a cool, yogurt dressing.

10 minutes preparation
10 minutes cooking

Ingredients for 2

1 cup lean ground lamb
1 small onion, peeled and finely chopped
1 clove garlic, chopped
½ tsp ground cilantro
2 tbsp fresh mint, chopped
salt
black pepper, freshly ground

To serve

2 pita breads
mixed green salad leaves
bought tzatziki dressing

Ingredients for 4

2 cups lean ground lamb
1 onion, peeled and finely chopped
1 clove garlic, chopped
1 tsp ground cilantro
4 tbsp fresh mint, chopped
salt
black pepper, freshly ground

To serve

4 pita breads
mixed green salad leaves
bought tzatziki dressing

1 Preheat the broiler to high. Soak wooden skewers or have metal ones ready. Mix the lamb, onion, garlic, and herbs together, then season well with salt and black pepper.

2 Divide into 12 pieces and squeeze each piece around the skewers in a flat ball shape.

3 Place under the broiler and broil for about 10 minutes, until browned all over, turning regularly.

4 Warm the pita breads under the broiler, open and fill with salad leaves. Add the lamb koftas. drizzle with tzatziki dressing, and then serve immediately.

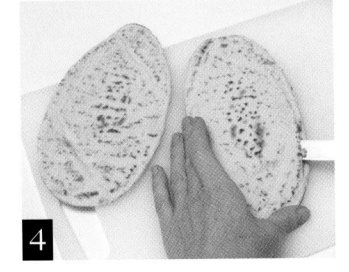

Lemon & Pork Patties

Freezer Friendly

These crisp little patties have a fresh, lemony tang. If you make double the amount, you can store some in the freezer.

Ingredients for 2

½ **lemon**
1 **cup lean ground pork**
1 **green onion, finely**
   chopped
¼ **tsp dried sage**
1 **tsp soy sauce**
salt
black pepper, freshly ground
1 **tbsp all-purpose flour**
1¾ **tbsp butter**
½ **cup chicken stock**
1 **tsp cornstarch**

Ingredients for 4

1 **lemon**
2 **cups lean ground pork**
2 **green onions, finely**
   chopped
½ **tsp dried sage**
2 **tsp soy sauce**
salt
black pepper, freshly ground
2 **tbsp all-purpose flour**
¼ **cup butter**
1¼ **cups chicken stock**
2 **tsp cornstarch**

10 minutes preparation
15 minutes cooking

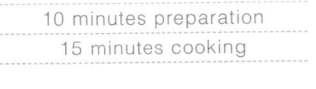

1 Finely grate the rind from the lemon into the ground pork and mix together with the onions, sage, and soy sauce.

2 Season with salt and black pepper, then shape into 4 (8) thin patties. Dust each one lightly with flour.

3 Heat the butter in a large nonstick skillet and fry the patties for 5 minutes on each side. Keep warm.

4 Blend 1 tablespoon of chicken stock to a paste with the cornstarch, then stir into the chicken stock and heat until thickened. Add 1 (2) teaspoon(s) of lemon juice and heat until thickened. Serve over the patties with broiled cherry tomatoes and green beans.

Spicy Chicken Teriyaki

Family Favorite

Prepare these spicy chicken pieces and leave them to marinate while you are out. You can broil them in just 10 minutes when you return.

Ingredients for 2

2 skinless, boneless chicken breasts
2 tbsp sesame seeds
1½ tbsp dark soy sauce
juice of ½ lime
½ tbsp dry sherry
½ tbsp sesame oil
1 tbsp clear honey
1 small clove garlic, chopped
1 tsp fresh ginger root, chopped

Ingredients for 4

4 skinless, boneless chicken breasts
4 tbsp sesame seeds
3 tbsp dark soy sauce
juice of 1 lime
1 tbsp dry sherry
1 tbsp sesame oil
2 tbsp clear honey
1 large clove garlic, chopped
2 tsp fresh ginger root, chopped

15 minutes preparation
10 minutes cooking

1 Cut the chicken into 1in cubes and thread on to 4 (8) skewers. Place the sesame seeds in a nonstick skillet and dry-fry over a low heat for 2–3 minutes, until toasted.

2 Place the sesame seeds and all the remaining ingredients in a shallow dish and then spoon over the chicken kabobs.

3 Cover the dish with plastic wrap and chill the kabobs for 10 minutes (or longer).

4 Heat the broiler to hot. Place the chicken on the broiler pan, keeping any marinade from the dish. Broil the kabobs for 10 minutes, turning frequently. Spoon the marinade over them as they cook. When they are ready, serve them with boiled noodles and stir-fried vegetables.

Vegetarian Meals

Penne With Broccoli

Quick and Easy

You'll only need one pan in which to prepare and cook this quick and easy supper

Ingredients for 2

6oz broccoli florets
7oz penne pasta
½ cup sun-dried tomatoes
   in oil
1 tbsp olive oil
3oz goat cheese
black pepper, freshly ground

Ingredients for 4

1lb broccoli florets
12oz penne pasta
¾ cup sun-dried tomatoes
   in oil
2 tbsp olive oil
6oz goat cheese
black pepper, freshly ground

10 minutes preparation
15 minutes cooking

1 Bring a large pan of salted water to the boil and cook the broccoli florets for 4 minutes, until tender.

2 Lift the broccoli from the pan with a slotted spoon and drain in a colander. Add the pasta to the same water in the pan and cook according to the package instructions until *al dente*. Drain well.

3 Return the pasta and broccoli to the pan. Drain the sun-dried tomatoes, chop coarsely, and add to the pan.

4 Toss together with the olive oil and divide between warmed serving bowls. Crumble over the goat cheese and serve immediately, seasoned with freshly ground black pepper.

Polenta With Ratatouille

Easy Entertaining

Making polenta from scratch is quite a lengthy process, but now that it is sold ready-made you simply slice, heat, and serve it.

Ingredients for 2

9oz ready-made polenta
1 tbsp olive oil
1 small red onion, peeled
1 medium-sized zuccini
1 small eggplant
1 clove garlic, peeled and chopped
6oz ripe cherry tomatoes on the vine
¼ cup mozzarella cheese, sliced

Ingredients for 4

1lb 2oz packet ready-made polenta
2 tbsp olive oil
1 medium-sized red onion, peeled
2 medium-sized zucchini
1 medium-sized eggplant
1 clove garlic, peeled and chopped
12oz ripe cherry tomatoes on the vine
½ cup mozzarella cheese, sliced

10 minutes preparation
12 minutes cooking

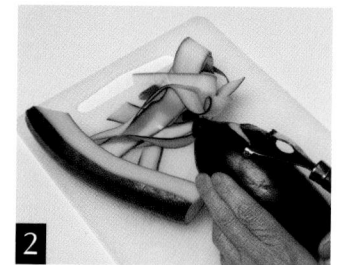

1 Cut the polenta into 1in-thick slices. Brush a heavy-based grill pan or skillet with half of the oil and fry the polenta for 3 minutes on each side until golden, turning once. Now place on a large cookie sheet.

2 Meanwhile, slice the onions into thin wedges. Top and tail the zucchini and eggplant and cut into ribbons by running a vegetable peeler down the vegetables.

3 Heat the remaining oil in the grill pan or skillet and fry the onion and garlic for 2 minutes. Add the zucchini and eggplant for 5 minutes.

4 Preheat the broiler. Broil the strings of tomatoes for 5 minutes, until softened and beginning to split. Pile the sliced vegetables on the polenta pieces. Broil for 2 minutes, add the sliced cheese, and broil for a further 2 minutes, until melting and bubbling. Serve with tossed green-leaf salad.

Two-bean Salad

Quick and Easy

This colorful salad is substantial enough to keep even any nonvegetarians happy. Serve it with chunks of sourdough or crusty, wholewheat bread.

Ingredients for 2

4 tbsp olive oil
2 green onions, finely sliced
1 clove garlic, chopped
½ red chile pepper, deseeded and chopped
1 stalk celery, finely chopped
1 small, green bell pepper, deseeded and finely diced
1 tsp dried oregano
7oz can cannellini beans
7oz can cranberry or red kidney beans
2 ripe tomatoes, diced
1 tbsp red-wine vinegar

Ingredients for 4

8 tbsp olive oil
4 green onions, finely sliced
2 cloves garlic, chopped
1 red chile pepper, deseeded and chopped
2 stalks celery, finely chopped
1 large, green bell pepper, deseeded and finely diced
2 tsp dried oregano
14oz can cannellini beans
14oz can cranberry or red kidney beans
4 ripe tomatoes, diced
2 tbsp red-wine vinegar

10 minutes preparation
10 minutes cooking

1 Heat 2 (4) tablespoons of the oil in a large pskilletan or wok and fry the onions, garlic, chile pepper, celery, bell pepper, and herbs over a medium heat for 6 minutes to soften the vegetables.

2 Drain the beans and rinse them under cold water. Add the beans to the skillet or wok and cook for 4 minutes.

3 Pour the contents of the skillet or wok into a large

bowl, add the diced tomatoes, and stir well.

4 Whisk the remaining oil with the vinegar and stir into the salad. Serve warm or cold on romaine lettuce leaves, sprinkled with fresh herbs.

Mushroom Risotto

Easy Entertaining

Risotto is a favorite in our house—it's such an easy supper to prepare, and you can always vary the ingredients

Ingredients for 2

- 1 tbsp butter
- 2 tsp olive oil
- 1 small onion, finely chopped
- 1 clove garlic, chopped
- 2 stalks celery, chopped
- ¾ cup arborio or risotto rice
- 9oz sliced mushrooms, such as chestnut, portobello or white
- ⅓ cup dry white wine
- 2 cups vegetable stock
- ¼ cup fresh Parmesan cheese, grated into curls
- 2 tbsp fresh basil, chopped

Ingredients for 4

- 1 ¾ tbsp butter
- 1 tbsp olive oil
- 1 onion, finely chopped
- 1 clove garlic, chopped
- 4 stalks celery, chopped
- 1⅓ cup arborio or risotto rice
- 1lb 2oz sliced mushrooms, such as chestnut, portobello or white
- ½ cup dry white wine
- 3 cups vegetable stock
- ½ cup fresh Parmesan cheese, grated into curls
- 2 tbsp fresh basil, chopped

10 minutes preparation
25 minutes cooking

1 Heat the butter and oil in a large sauté pan or deep skillet, add the onions, garlic, and celery and fry for 3 minutes to soften. Add the rice and stir-fry for 2 minutes to coat in the oil.

2 Add the mushrooms and stir-fry for 3 minutes. Mix the wine and stock together and pour a quarter of the liquid into the pan or skillet.

3 Simmer over a low heat until the liquid has been absorbed, then add another quarter of the liquid. Continue adding the liquid. When the rice has absorbed the last addition, it will be tender. This will take about 15–20 minutes.

4 Divide between warmed serving bowls and sprinkle with the the parmesan and basil before serving.

Cauliflower & Potato Curry

spicy

This Indian dish is also known as *aloo gobi* and is a favorite in our family. I like to serve it with a dish of dal, and some plain, boiled rice. Garnish it with flaked or curled coconut, available from health-food stores.

Ingredients for 2

- **1 small cauliflower**
- **2 tsp sunflower oil**
- **2 tsp black mustard seeds**
- **½ tsp ground turmeric**
- **1 cup potatoes, peeled and cubed**
- **¼ cup frozen peas**
- **1 chile pepper, deseeded and chopped**
- **small bunch fresh cilantro, chopped**
- **coconut flakes to serve**

Ingredients for 4

- **1 medium-sized cauliflower**
- **1 tbsp sunflower oil**
- **1 tbsp black mustard seeds**
- **½ tsp ground turmeric**
- **2 cups potatoes, peeled and cubed**
- **½ cup frozen peas**
- **2 chile peppers, deseeded and chopped**
- **large bunch fresh cilantro, chopped**
- **coconut flakes to serve**

10 minutes preparation
24 minutes cooking

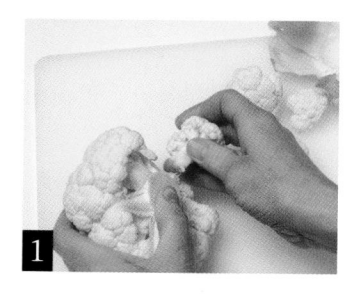

1 Break the cauliflower into florets and add to a large pan of boiling, salted water. Boil for 2 minutes then drain.

2 Heat the oil in a large skillet or wok and add the mustard seeds and turmeric. Fry for 1 minute, then add the potatoes and stir-fry for 1 minute to coat the cubes in the spices.

3 Add ½ cup (1¼ cups) of water, stir, cover with a lid or piece of aluminum foil and cook for 10 minutes.

4 Add the peas, chile peppers, and cauliflower, cover, and cook for 10 minutes until the vegetables are soft and the liquid has reduced. Fold in the cilantro and serve sprinkled with coconut flakes.

Vegetarian Chili

Family Favorite

Chili is always a quick favorite, but don't worry if you don't have the right combination of vegetables: just use up whatever you can find in the vegetable bin and freezer—it always works out!

10 minutes preparation

24 minutes cooking

Ingredients for 2

- 1 tbsp sunflower oil
- 1 small red onion, chopped
- 1 clove garlic, peeled and chopped
- 1 chile pepper, deseeded and finely chopped
- ½ tsp chile powder
- ½ tsp cumin seeds
- ½ cup bottled red peppers, drained and sliced
- 1 large carrot, diced
- 2 stalks celery, sliced
- ½ cup mushrooms, chopped
- ½ cup tomato passata sauce
- 14oz can red kidney beans

Ingredients for 4

- 2 tbsp sunflower oil
- 1 large red onion, chopped
- 2 cloves garlic, peeled and chopped
- 2 chile peppers, deseeded and finely chopped
- 1 tsp chilli powder
- 1 tsp cumin seeds
- 1 cup bottled red peppers, drained and sliced
- 2 large carrots, diced
- 4 stalks celery, sliced
- 1 cup mushrooms, chopped
- 1¼ cups tomato passata sauce
- 2 x 14oz cans red kidney beans

1 Heat the oil in a large skillet or wok and stir fry the onion, garlic, and chile for 2 minutes.

2 Add the chile powder, cumin seeds, and peppers and cook for a further 2 minutes, stirring constantly.

3 Add the carrots, celery, and mushrooms and stir-fry for 2 minutes. Add the passata and ½ cup (1 cup) of water and cook, covered, for 10 minutes, until the vegetables are soft.

4 Drain the beans, rinse under cold water, then add to the skillet or wok and cook for 10 minutes, until hot. Add the cilantro and serve in tacos, or with plain rice.

Couscous & Fava-bean Salad

Easy Entertaining

This salad is ideal for hot, summer days. You can make it well ahead of time, and keep it chilled in the fridge until needed.

Ingredients for 2

½ cup couscous
½ cup frozen fava beans
½ cup frozen peas
1 large beefstake tomato
2 tbsp olive oil
1 small red onion, finely
　chopped
2 tbsp fresh mint, chopped
1 tbsp fresh Italian parsley,
　chopped
salt
black pepper, freshly ground
A few arugula leaves
¼ cup feta cheese,
　chopped

Ingredients for 4

1 cup couscous
1 cup frozen fava beans
1 cup frozen peas
2 large beefstake tomatoes
4 tbsp olive oil
1 medium-sized red onion,
　finely chopped
4 tbsp fresh mint, chopped
2 tbsp fresh Italian parsley,
　chopped
salt
black pepper, freshly ground
A few arugula leaves
½ cup feta cheese,
　chopped

10 minutes preparation
15 minutes cooking

1 Put the couscous in a large bowl and stir in ½ cup (1¼ cups) boiling water. (If you have quick-cook couscous, follow the intsructions on the package.) Stir until absorbed then stand for 15 minutes, until the grains are tender. Fluff up the grains with a fork.

2 Cook the fava beans and peas in boiling, salted water for 4 minutes, until tender, and drain the vegetables in a colander. If the skins of the beans are thick, peel them away while still warm. Add the green centers to the couscous with the peas.

3 Cut the tomatoes in half, scoop out the seeds, and discard them. Chop the flesh finely into dice and add to the couscous with the olive oil, onion, and chopped herbs. Then stir together using a large, metal spoon.

4 Season with salt and freshly ground black pepper, then spoon the salad on to a bed of arugula on a serving dish. Crumble the feta cheese and sprinkle over the top of the salad before serving.

Macaroni & Cauliflower Cheese

Quick and Easy

I live in a part of the country where cauliflowers are grown, so we tend to eat lots of them. This is always a family favorite

Ingredients for 2

½ cup macaroni or rigatoni pasta
12oz cauliflower, broken into small florets
1½ tbsp butter, softened, plus a little extra
1½ tbsp all-purpose flour
1¼ cups milk
⅓ cup Cheddar cheese, grated
½ tsp French mustard
salt
black pepper, freshly ground
1¾ tbsp brown breadcrumbs

Ingredients for 4

¾ cup macaroni or rigatoni pasta
1lb 4oz cauliflower, broken into small florets
2¾ tbsp butter, softened, plus a little extra
2¾ tbsp all-purpose flour
2½ cups milk
¾ cup Cheddar cheese, grated
1 tsp French mustard
salt
black pepper, freshly ground
¼ cup brown breadcrumbs

10 minutes preparation
15 minutes cooking

1 Bring a large, deep pan of boiling, salted water to the boil and cook the pasta according to the package instructions. Add the cauliflower florets to the same pan of water for the last 8 minutes of the pasta's cooking time and cook until tender. Drain both the pasta and cauliflower to remove any extra liquid, then transfer to a buttered, heatproof dish.

2 Meanwhile, make the sauce. Put the butter, flour, and milk in a heavy based pan and heat gently, whisking constantly until the mixture thickens. Simmer for 3 minutes then add half of the cheese and season with mustard, salt, and pepper. Heat the broiler.

3 Pour the sauce over the pasta and cauliflower in the dish and sprinkle the breadcrumbs and the remaining cheese evenly over the top.

4 Place the dish under a hot broiler and broil for 2–4 minutes, until the top is browned and bubbling. Remove from the broiler, holding the dish with oven mitts as it will be very hot.

Cook's Tip:

This dish freezes well. Prepare up to the end of step 3, but don't broil the topping. Cool and freeze in the dish. Wrap in aluminum foil and freeze for up to 2 months. To use, defrost, then reheat in a microwave oven for 2-3 minutes, or in an oven set to 375°F for 15-20 minutes. Finally, finish the topping under the broiler.

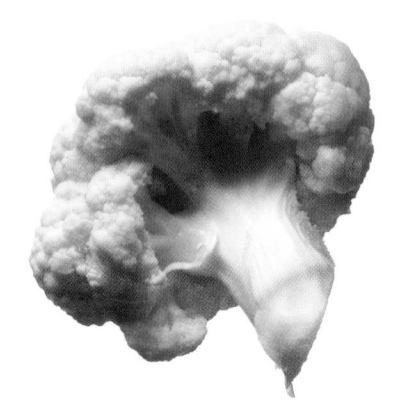

Cannellini-bean & Artichoke Salad

vegetarian

This colorful and delicate salad can also be served in smaller portions as an appetizer.

Ingredients for 2

14oz can cannellini or
 flageolet beans, drained
3 green onions, finely sliced
5oz jar charbroiled
 artichokes in oil
2 tbsp fresh basil
5oz baby vine tomatoes
olive oil
½ tbsp white-wine vinegar
salt
black pepper, freshly ground
a few salad leaves
1¾ tbsp pine nuts

Ingredients for 4

2 x 14oz cans cannellini
 or flageolet beans, drained
6 green onions, finely sliced
10oz jar charbroiled
 artichokes in oil
4 tbsp fresh basil
10oz baby vine tomatoes
olive oil
1 tbsp white-wine vinegar
salt
black pepper, freshly ground
a few salad leaves
¼ cup pine nuts

10 minutes preparation
No cooking

1 Place the beans in a bowl with the onions. Lift the artichokes from the jar, reserving the oil, and cut into quarters.

2 Chop the basil into fine shreds and halve the tomatoes. Add to the bowl.

3 Measure the oil from the jar with enough olive oil to make up to 3 (6) tablespoonfuls. Mix with the vinegar and then season with salt and pepper to make a light dressing.

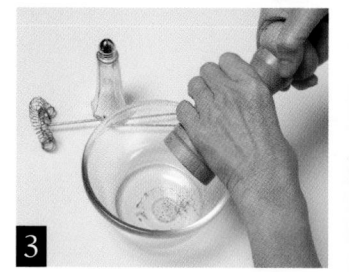

4 Toss the salad ingredients together with the dressing. Line 2 (4) serving plates with salad leaves and spoon the salad on top. Sprinkle with pine nuts to serve.

Thai Vegetable Rice

Low Fat

This recipe uses sticky Thai jasmine rice that can be cooked ahead of time and reheated.

Ingredients for 2

- ½ cup jasmine rice
- 1 tbsp sunflower oil
- 4 green onions, finely chopped
- 1 clove garlic, chopped
- 1in-piece fresh ginger root, peeled and chopped
- 2 tsp Thai green-curry paste
- ½ cup mushrooms, sliced
- 4oz pack stir-fry frozen Chinese vegetables
- 2 tsp soy sauce

Ingredients for 4

- 1 cup jasmine rice
- 2 tbsp sunflower oil
- 8 green onions, finely chopped
- 2 cloves garlic, chopped
- 2in-piece fresh ginger root, peeled and chopped
- 1 tbsp Thai green-curry paste
- ¾ cup mushrooms, sliced
- 8oz pack stir-fry frozen Chinese vegetables
- 1 tbsp soy sauce

10 minutes preparation
10 minutes cooking

1 Cook the rice according to the package instructions and drain well. (The rice can be cooked ahead and cooled if this is more convenient.)

2 Heat the oil in a wok or large skillet and add half of the green onions. Add the garlic and ginger and stir-fry for 1 minute, then add the green-curry paste and cook for 1 minute.

3 Add the mushrooms and stir-fry for 1 minute, then add the frozen vegetables and stir-fry for 3–4 minutes, until they are thawed and tender.

4 Add the rice and stir-fry for 2 minutes, until heated thoroughly, then stir in the soy sauce. Sprinkle with the remaining green onions before serving.

Cheesy Leek Pasta

Family Favorite

Pasta with a light vegetable topping makes an ideal supper dish for all the family.

10 minutes preparation
12 minutes cooking

Ingredients for 2

6oz tagliatelle pasta
9oz leeks
2 tbsp olive oil
1 clove garlic, peeled and
  chopped
¼ cup white mushrooms,
  sliced
2 tbsp capers
Finely grated zest and juice
  of ½ lemon
¼ cup whole-wheat bread,
  diced
¼ cup Edam cheese,
  grated

Ingredients for 4

12oz tagliatelle pasta
1lb 2oz leeks
4 tbsp olive oil
2 cloves garlic, peeled and
  chopped
½ cup white mushrooms,
  sliced
4 tbsp capers
Finely grated zest and juice
  of 1 lemon
½ cup whole-wheat bread,
  diced
½ cup Edam cheese,
  grated

1 Cook the pasta ribbons in a large pan of boiling, salted water according to the package instructions.

2 Meanwhile, trim the leeks and almost slice in half down to the root. Swirl in cold water to remove any grit or dirt, then slice thinly.

3 Heat half of the oil in a large skillet or wok and fry the garlic with the leeks until tender for 5 minutes, stirring.

Add the mushrooms, capers, lemon zest, and juice and stir-fry for 3 minutes.

4 Fry the cubes of bread in the remaining oil for 4 minutes, until crisp. Drain the cooked pasta and stir with the leek mixture. Place on serving plates and top with hot croutons and grated cheese.

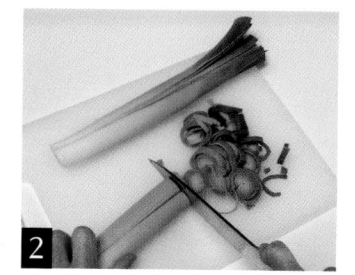

Gnocchi With a Rich Tomato Sauce

Quick and Easy

Ready-prepared potato gnocchi, sold in sealed packs, takes only minutes to cook. These creamy potato balls coated in a rich, red sauce make an ideal last-minute supper dish.

Ingredients for 2

- **14oz package potato gnocchi**
- **4oz jar roasted red peppers, drained**
- **2 tbsp sun-dried-tomato pesto**
- **7oz can diced tomatoes in tomato juice**
- **¼ tsp dried red-pepper flakes**
- **1 tbsp fresh basil**
- **salt**
- **black pepper, freshly ground**
- **1¾ tbsp breadcrumbs**
- **¼ cup Edam cheese, grated**

Ingredients for 4

- **2 x 14oz packs potato gnocchi**
- **7oz jar roasted red peppers, drained**
- **4 tbsp sun-dried-tomato pesto**
- **14oz can diced tomatoes in tomato juice**
- **½ tsp dried red-pepper flakes**
- **2 tbsp fresh basil**
- **salt**
- **black pepper, freshly ground**
- **¼ cup breadcrumbs**
- **½ cup Edam cheese, grated**

5 minutes preparation

5 minutes cooking

1 Bring a large pan of salted water to a boil, add the gnocchi, and cook for 2–3 minutes, or according to the package instructions, until tender. Drain the gnocchi in a large colander and place in a buttered, heatproof dish. Preheat the broiler to its highest setting.

2 Place the peppers, pesto, and canned tomatoes in a small food processor or blender with the red-pepper flakes and basil. Measure out 3 (6) tablespoons of cold water add to the food processor or blender. Now process or blend to a smooth sauce for about 30 seconds.

3 Place the sauce in a small pan and heat to just below boiling. Stir the sauce well, season with salt and ground pepper, then pour over the gnocchi. Try to make sure that all the pieces of gnocchi are coated with the sauce.

4 Sprinkle the breadcrumbs and grated Edam cheese evenly over the top of the gnocchi. Broil for 3 minutes until bubbling and browned. Serve immediately, spooned on to serving plates with a green salad and crusty bread.

Tomato Rice With Red Kidney Beans

From the Pantry

When you don't have time to shop, make this quick supper from ingredients in the pantry.

Ingredients for 2

- 1 tbsp sunflower oil
- 1 small onion, peeled and chopped
- 1 clove garlic, peeled and chopped
- 1 small green bell pepper, deseeded and diced
- 2 tsp paprika
- ½ cup easy-cook rice
- 7oz can diced tomatoes
- salt
- 7oz can red kidney beans
- 1 tbsp fresh cilantro, chopped

Ingredients for 4

- 2 tbsp sunflower oil
- 1 large onion, peeled and chopped
- 1 clove garlic, peeled and chopped
- 1 green bell pepper, deseeded and diced
- 1 tbsp paprika
- 1 cup easy-cook rice
- 14oz can diced tomatoes
- salt
- 14oz can red kidney beans
- 2 tbsp fresh cilantro, chopped

5 minutes preparation
20 minutes cooking

1 Heat the sunflower oil in a large, deep, heavy-based pan for about 30 seconds. Add the onion, garlic, and bell pepper and cook for about 3 minutes over a medium heat, until the onions and pepper are slightly softened. Don't let the heat get too high, or the onions may start to burn.

2 Add the paprika and cook for 1 minute, stirring frequently with a wooden spoon. Add the rice and cook for 1 minute, stirring over a moderate heat to coat the grains of rice.

3 Pour the tomatoes into a measuring pitcher and bring the level up to 1¼ cups (2½ cups) with cold water. Add to the rice in the pan and season with a little salt. Cook,

covered with a lid or a piece of aluminum foil to keep in the heat for 15 minutes.

4 Drain and rinse the beans in a colander. Add to the pan 5 minutes before the end of the cooking time and cook until the rice is tender and all of the liquid has been absorbed. Sprinkle with fresh cilantro and serve with a dish of plain yogurt and a fresh, green salad

Bean Burgers

spicy

You can make and shape these patties ahead of time—they make a popular alternative to regular hamburgers for nonmeat-eaters at barbecues.

Ingredients for 2

1 tbsp olive oil
1 clove garlic, chopped
1 small red onion, peeled and chopped
14oz can navy or lima beans
¼ tsp dried red-pepper flakes
½ tsp cumin seeds
1 large egg, beaten
1¾ tsp sharp Cheddar cheese, grated
salt
black pepper, freshly ground
1 tbsp all-purpose flour
2¾ tbsp breadcrumbs

Ingredients for 4

2 tbsp olive oil
2 cloves garlic, chopped
1 medium-sized red onion, peeled and chopped
14oz cans navy or lima beans
½ tsp dried red-pepper flakes
1 tsp cumin seeds
2 eggs, beaten
¼ cup sharp Cheddar cheese, grated
salt
black pepper, freshly ground
1 tbsp all-purpose flour
1/3 cup breadcrumbs

10 minutes preparation
8 minutes cooking

1 Heat 2 teaspoons of the oil in a small skillet, fry the garlic and onion until softened, then place in a bowl and cool.

2 Drain and rinse the beans and place in a food processor with the red-pepper flakes, cumin seeds, and half of the egg. Process until the beans are smooth, then put in the bowl with the onions. Add the cheese, season with salt and ground pepper, and mix to a paste.

3 Divide the mixture into 4 (8) neat, flat patties. Dust in the flour. Beat the remaining egg in a small bowl and spread out the breadcrumbs on a plate. Dip the patties in egg then roll in the crumbs.

4 Heat the oil in a nonstick skillet and fry for 4 minutes on each side, until golden. Serve in split, toasted buns accompanied by salad and mayonnaise.

Vegetable & Cheese Bake

Family Favorite

I make this simple family favorite as a midweek supper dish from the pantry and vegetable bin. If you don't have the right combination of vegetables, just improvise!

Ingredients for 2

6oz carrots
8oz small new potatoes,
  unpeeled
1 tbsp butter
1 small onion, chopped
½ cup zucchini, sliced
3oz frozen green beans
¼ cup garlic and herb
  cream cheese
¼ cup Greek-style yogurt
1¾ tbsp Cheddar cheese,
  grated

Ingredients for 4

12oz carrots
1lb small new potatoes,
  unpeeled
1¾ tbsp butter
1 medium-sized onion,
  chopped
1 cup zucchini, sliced
6oz frozen green beans
½ cup garlic and herb
  cream cheese
½ cup Greek-style yogurt
¼ cup Cheddar cheese,
  grated

15 minutes preparation
15 minutes cooking

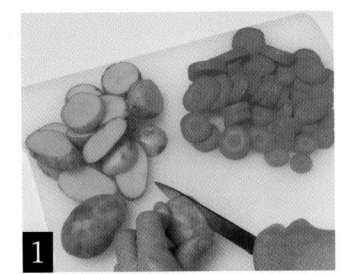

1

1 Preheat the oven to 350°F. Scrub and slice the carrots and potatoes, boil in salted water for 5 minutes, and then drain.

2 Melt the butter and fry the onion to soften for 2 minutes then add the sliced zucchini and beans, and stir-fry for 2 minutes.

3 Reduce the heat before stirring in the cream cheese, thick yogurt, and drained vegetables.

4 Transfer to an ovenproof dish and sprinkle the cheese over the top. Bake for 15 minutes, until the vegetables are tender and the top is golden.

2

3

Tricolor Pasta

Easy Entertaining

I am a fan of the fresh pastas sold in supermarkets and delis as they take only 2-3 minutes to cook and have a lovely, soft texture.

Ingredients for 2

1 tbsp olive oil
1 small onion, chopped
1 small clove garlic, peeled
  and chopped
½ red bell pepper, deseeded
  and chopped
7oz can diced tomatoes
4oz haricot verts, halved
1 cup fresh pasta shells,
  twists, or bows
6oz small spinach
  leaves
¼ cup feta cheese
2 tbsp fresh basil leaves,
  chopped

Ingredients for 4

2 tbsp olive oil
1 medium-sized onion,
  chopped
1 large clove garlic, peeled
  and chopped
1 red bell pepper, deseeded
  and chopped
14oz can diced tomatoes
7oz haricot verts, halved
2 cups fresh pasta shells,
  twists, or bows
12oz small spinach
  leaves
½ cup feta cheese
4 tbsp fresh basil leaves,
  chopped

10 minutes preparation
12 minutes cooking

1 Heat the oil in a large skillet. Add the onion, garlic, and bell pepper and cook for 5 minutes to soften. Add the tomatoes and cook for a further 3 minutes.

2 Place a large pan of salted water on to boil, add the haricot verts, and cook for 6 minutes. For the last 3 minutes of cooking time, add the fresh pasta. Then drain the pasta and haricot verts in a colander.

3 Wash and drain the spinach leaves and remove any tough stalks. Add to the sauce and cook for 3 minutes until they wilt. Toss the pasta and sauce together.

4 Divide the pasta between warmed serving bowls. Crumble over the feta cheese and chopped basil and serve with chunks of crusty bread,

Three-layer Salad

No cooking

As this tasty salad is made from bright, colorful layers, it appeals to children, as well as adults—it's a great way of getting them to eat more healthily.

Ingredients for 4

20 minutes preparation

No cooking

Layer 1

1 cup bulgur
1 tbsp fresh Italian parsley, chopped
1 tbsp fresh mint, chopped
finely grated zest and juice of 1 lemon
4 tbsp olive oil
2 green onions, finely chopped

Layer 2

14oz can garbanzos, washed and drained
12oz carrots, peeled and grated
¼ cup raisins
finely grated zest and juice of 1 orange
2 tbsp olive oil

Layer 3

3 tbsp olive oil
1 tbsp white-wine vinegar
1 tsp mustard
14oz can red kidney beans, washed and drained
2 stalks celery, chopped
1 package mixed salad leaves

1 Put the bulgur in a bowl and cover with ¾ cup of boiling water and leave to stand for 10 minutes. Add the remaining ingredients for layer 1 and toss together.

2 Wash and drain the garbanzos and toss with all the ingredients for layer 2 in a large bowl.

3 Mix the olive oil, vinegar, and mustard together in a small jar, then toss together with the ingredients for layer 3.

4 Place the bulgur layer in the base of a large, glass serving dish. Place the carrot layer on top of this. Top with the red kidney bean and salad layer. Serve with crusty bread.

Vegetable Stir-fry

Low Fat

Stir-fries are always a favorite, and this one is so superquick to make that the vegetables stay crisp and crunchy. You can make your own combination of vegetables, providing that they are all chopped finely enough to cook together.

Ingredients for 2

- 1 tbsp sunflower oil
- 1 clove garlic, peeled and chopped
- 1in-piece fresh ginger root, peeled and chopped
- 1 small onion, thinly sliced
- ¼ cup carrots, peeled and cut into matchsticklike pieces
- ½ cup cremini or chestnut mushrooms, sliced
- 3oz baby corn
- ½ cup mung bean sprouts
- 4oz young spinach, washed
- 1 tbsp lemon juice
- 2 tsp clear honey
- 2 tbsp teriyaki sauce

Ingredients for 4

- 2 tbsp sunflower oil
- 2 cloves garlic, peeled and chopped
- 2in-piece fresh ginger root, peeled and chopped
- 1 onion, thinly sliced
- ½ cup carrots, peeled and cut into matchsticklike pieces
- 1 cup cremini or chestnut mushrooms, sliced
- 6oz baby corn
- 1 cup mung bean sprouts
- 8oz young spinach, washed
- 2 tbsp lemon juice
- 1 tbsp clear honey
- 4 tbsp teriyaki sauce

15 minutes preparation

5 minutes cooking

1 Heat the oil in a wok or a large skillet, add the garlic, ginger, and onion, and stir-fry for 1 minute.

2 Add the carrots, mushrooms, and baby corn and stir-fry for 3 minutes, or until the vegetables begin to soften.

3 Add the mung bean sprouts and cook for 1 minute. Add the spinach and stir-fry for 1 minute, until the leaves begin to wilt.

4 Mix the lemon juice, honey, and sauce together in a small pitcher then pour in the wok or skillet and stir-fry to coat the vegetables. Serve at once with boiled rice noodles.

Lemon Dal

Freezer Friendly

Make a double batch of this spicy Indian dish and keep half in the freezer for another day.
Serve it with a vegetarian curry and Indian breads and relishes.

5 minutes preparation
25 minutes cooking

Ingredients for 2

- 2 tsp sunflower oil
- 1 small onion, peeled and chopped
- 1 clove garlic, peeled and chopped
- 1in-piece fresh ginger root, peeled and chopped
- ½ green jalapeno pepper, deseeded and finely chopped
- ½ tsp black mustard seeds
- ½ tsp ground cumin
- ½ tsp ground cardamom seeds
- ½ tsp ground turmeric
- ½ cup red or yellow split lentils
- 1¾ cups vegetable stock
- finely grated zest and juice of ½ lemon

Ingredients for 4

- 1 tbsp sunflower oil
- 1 large onion, peeled and chopped
- 2 cloves garlic, peeled and chopped
- 2in-fresh ginger root, peeled and chopped
- 1 green jalapeno pepper, deseeded and finely chopped
- 1 tsp black mustard seeds
- 1 tsp ground cumin
- 1 tsp ground cardamom seeds
- 1 tsp ground turmeric
- 1 cup red or yellow split lentils
- 3 cups vegetable stock
- Finely grated zest and juice of 1 lemon

1 Heat the oil in a large, heavy-based saucepan. Add the onion, garlic, ginger and jalapeno pepper and cook for 3 minutes to soften.

2 Add all of the spices to the pan and cook for 2 minutes, until the mustard seeds pop.

3 Wash the lentils thoroughly, checking for any pieces of grit. Add the drained lentils and stock to the pan, cover, and simmer gently for 15–20 minutes, until thick and mushy.

4 Add the lemon rind and juice and cook for a further 5 minutes. Serve with popadoms, boiled rice, and a vegetable curry.

Lima-bean Stew

Low Fat

This is a quick version of a bean dish that is commonly eaten in Greece during the Lenten period before Easter.

Ingredients for 2

- 1 tbsp olive oil
- 1 shallot, chopped
- 1 stalk celery, sliced
- 1 clove garlic, peeled and chopped
- 7oz can diced tomatoes
- ¼ tsp paprika
- ½ cup vegetable stock
- 14oz can lima beans
- 1 sprig fresh oregano or 1 tsp dried oregano
- salt
- black pepper, freshly ground
- 1 tbsp fresh Italian parsley, chopped

Ingredients for 4

- 2 tbsp olive oil
- 2 shallots, chopped
- 2 stalks celery, sliced
- 2 cloves garlic, peeled and chopped
- 14oz can diced tomatoes
- ½ tsp paprika
- 1 cup vegetable stock
- 2 x 14oz cans lima beans
- 1 sprig fresh oregano or 1 tsp dried oregano
- salt
- black pepper, freshly ground
- 2 tbsp fresh flat leaf parsley, chopped

5 minutes preparation

20 minutes cooking

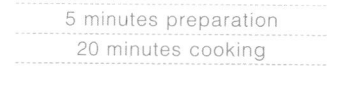

1 Heat the oil in a large skillet and fry the shallots, celery, and garlic for 3 minutes to soften.

2 Add the tomatoes, paprika, and stock to the skillet and stir together. Drain and rinse the beans under cold running water.

3 Add the beans to the skillet with the oregano and season with salt and freshly ground black pepper.

4 Simmer, covered, for 15 minutes, until the mixture thickens. Sprinkle with chopped parsley and serve with crusty bread.

Entertaining

Gingered Pork Fillet

Low Fat

Stir-frying is not only very quick and easy, it is a healthy way of cooking, too. As the food cooks so speedily, more vitamins and minerals are retained.

Ingredients for 2

10oz pork tenderloin fillet
2 tbsp soy sauce
½ tbsp sesame oil
1in-piece fresh ginger root, peeled and chopped
1 clove garlic, finely chopped
1 tsp peanut or sunflower oil
6oz mixed Chinese stir-fry vegetables, fresh or frozen
½ head Chinese bok choy
1 tsp toasted sesame seeds

Ingredients for 4

10oz pork tenderloin fillets
4 tbsp soy sauce
1 tbsp sesame oil
/2in-piece fresh ginger root, peeled and chopped
1 clove garlic, finely chopped
2 tsp peanut or sunflower oil
12oz mixed Chinese stir-fry vegetables, fresh or frozen
1 head Chinese bok choy
2 tsp toasted sesame seeds

5 minutes preparation
5 minutes chilling
10 minutes cooking

1 Slice the pork fillet thickly and place in a dish with the soy sauce, sesame oil, ginger, and garlic. Stir together and chill for 5 minutes.

2 Heat the oil in a wok or a large skillet. Remove the pork from the marinade with a slotted spoon. Fry the pork for 4 minutes, until browned all over. Remove from the wok or skillet and keep warm.

3 Add the vegetables to the wok or skillet with any remaining marinade from the dish and stir-fry for 3 minutes.

4 Return the pork fillets to the wok or skillet and stir-fry for 3 minutes until hot, then sprinkle with sesame seeds and serve with boiled noodles.

Herby Crusted Fish

Easy Entertaining

Fresh white fish coated in a crunchy topping with a tang of fresh herbs and lemon zest makes an ideal simple lunch or supper-party dish.

Ingredients for 2

**2 x 6oz thick cod or
    haddock fillets, skinned**
salt
white pepper
**1 tbsp fresh white
    breadcrumbs**
**1 tbsp fresh Italian parsley,
    finely chopped**
finely grated zest of ½ lemon
a few drops Tabasco sauce
2 tbsp olive oil
**1 cup frozen spinach,
    chopped**

Ingredients for 4

**4 x 6oz thick cod or
    haddock fillets, skinned**
salt
white pepper
**1¾ tbsp fresh white
    breadcrumbs**
**2 tbsp fresh Italian parsley,
    finely chopped**
finely grated zest of 1 lemon
a few drops Tabasco sauce
4 tbsp olive oil
**2 cups frozen spinach,
    chopped**

12 minutes preparation
14 minutes cooking

1 Preheat the oven to 400°F. Season the fish on both sides with salt and white pepper and lay on a greased cookie tray.

2 Mix the breadcrumbs together with the parsley, lemon zest, Tabasco, and oil in a small bowl.

3 Spoon the mixture on top of the fish and press it on to each fillet lightly to make it stick. Bake for 14 minutes, until the topping is browned and crusty and the fish is white and flakes easily.

4 Meanwhile, cook the frozen spinach in a little water for 3 minutes, drain, and press out the water through a fine sieve. Divide into 2 (4) small piles and place on serving plates. Slide each piece of cooked fish on top with a slotted spatula. Serve with baby boiled potatoes and lemon wedges.

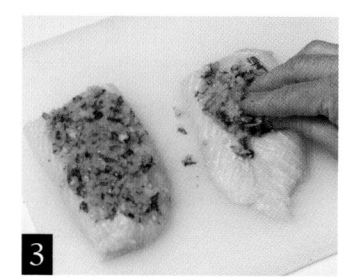

Duck & Honey Stir-fry

Easy Entertaining

Oriental flavors combine in this quickly cooked dish that makes an ideal entrée for a supper party.

Ingredients for 2

2 duck breasts
1 tbsp clear honey
2 tbsp soy sauce
1 tsp sesame oil
2 carrots
4 green onions
½ head bok choy
1 tbsp sunflower oil

Ingredients for 4

4 duck breasts
2 tbsp clear honey
4 tbsp soy sauce
2 tsp sesame oil
4 carrots
8 green onions
1 small head bok choy
2 tbsp sunflower oil

15 minutes preparation
10 minutes cooking

1 Slice the duck breasts thinly and place in a bowl. Mix the honey, soy sauce, and sesame oil together, add to the bowl, and then chill for 5–10 minutes.

2 Cut the carrots into fine matchsticks. Slice the onions and bok choy thinly.

3 Heat the oil in a wok or a large skillet. Drain the duck strips and stir-fry for 3 minutes, until browned. Then remove to a plate and   keep warm.

4 Add the sliced vegetables and stir-fry for 4 minutes. Return the duck to the wok or skillet with the marinade and stir-fry for a further 2 minutes, until hot. Serve with boiled egg noodles.

Minted Lamb Fillets

Low Fat

Fresh lamb fillets are well worth buying as they are lean and tender and cook much more quickly than lamb chops.

Ingredients for 2

2 x 5oz lamb fillets
2 tsp French mustard
1 tsp red-currant jelly
1 small clove garlic, peeled
and crushed
1 tbsp olive oil
2 tbsp fresh mint, chopped
1 tsp clear honey
1 tbsp sherry vinegar
1 tbsp capers, drained
½ tsp Worcestershire sauce

Ingredients for 4

4 x 5oz lamb fillets
4 tsp French mustard
2 tsp red-currant jelly
1 clove garlic, peeled and
crushed
2 tbsp olive oil
4 tbsp fresh mint, chopped
2 tsp clear honey
2 tbsp sherry vinegar
2 tbsp capers, drained
1 tsp Worcestershire sauce

12 minutes preparation

8 minutes cooking

1 Place the fillets on a plate and spread thinly with the mustard, jelly, and crushed garlic. Chill for 5 minutes. Heat a broiler to high.

2 Broil the lamb fillets on all sides for 10–12 minutes, until browned and seared all over. Keep warm on a serving platter.

3 Place the oil, mint, honey, vinegar, capers, and Worcestershire sauce in a small processor and blend until finely chopped.

4 Using a sharp knife, cut the lamb into 1in-thick slices. Place, overlapping, on serving plates and drizzle with the dressing. Serve with baby new potatoes and green peas.

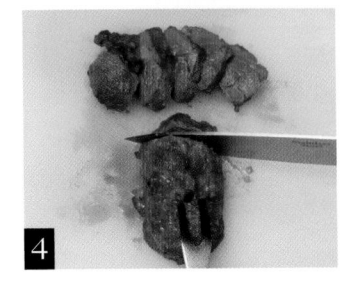

Salmon Steaks With Lemon Butter

Easy Entertaining

Lemon and fresh basil provide a delicious fresh topping for salmon steaks, and also help to keep the fish moist during baking.

10 minutes preparation

15 minutes cooking

Ingredients for 2

2 x 5oz salmon steaks
salt
white pepper
½ lemon
1¾ tbsp butter, softened
1 tbsp fresh basil, chopped
½ tbsp fresh parsley,
   chopped

Ingredients for 4

4 x 5oz salmon steaks
salt
white pepper
1 lemon
¼ cup butter, softened
2 tbsp fresh basil, chopped
1 tbsp fresh parsley,
   chopped

1 Preheat the oven to 400°F. Season the fish with salt and white pepper and place in a single layer in a greased, ovenproof dish.

2 Grate the zest finely from the lemon and then beat into the butter with the chopped herbs.

3 Spread the butter over each salmon steak. Cover with aluminum foil and and bake for 15 minutes, until the fish is tender.

4 Place the salmon on warmed serving plates and spoon over the melted butter from the dish. Serve with new potatoes and steamed snow peas or asparagus tips.

Shrimp Jambalaya

spicy

Adding giant shrimp to this spicy Southern rice-and-sausage dish results in a colorful and tempting supper.

5 minutes preparation

22 minutes cooking

Ingredients for 2

- 1 tbsp sunflower oil
- 2oz chorizo sausage, sliced
- 2 green onions, sliced
- 1 small clove garlic, peeled and chopped
- 1 small green bell pepper, deseeded and diced
- 2 stalks celery, sliced
- ½ tsp paprika
- ¼ tsp chile powder
- ½ tsp dried oregano
- ½ cup long-grain rice
- 1¼ cups hot chicken stock
- 9oz large, raw shrimp, heads removed

Ingredients for 4

- 2 tbsp sunflower oil
- 4oz chorizo sausage, sliced
- 4 green onions, sliced
- 1 clove garlic, peeled and chopped
- 1 large green bell pepper, deseeded and diced
- 4 stalks celery, sliced
- 1 tsp paprika
- ½ tsp chile powder
- 1 tsp dried oregano
- ¾ cup long-grain rice
- 2½ cups hot chicken stock
- 1lb 2oz large, raw shrimp, heads removed

1 Heat the oil in a large, deep skillet and fry the chorizo sausage until browned, for about 3 minutes.

2 Add the onions, garlic, bell pepper, and celery and cook over a medium heat for 5 minutes to soften.

3 Add the paprika, chile powder, and oregano and cook for 1 minute. Stir, then add the rice. Add the stock, stir, cover, and then simmer for 10 minutes.

4 Add the raw shrimp, stir into the rice, and cook for a further 5 minutes or until all of the liquid has been absorbed. Serve with a crisp, green salad.

Thai Beef Salad

Family Favorite

Don't be tempted to overcook the beef for this Thai recipe—it needs to be just seared.

10 minutes preparation

5 minutes cooking

Ingredients for 2

2oz rice noodles
1 tbsp crushed Szechwan
  peppercorns
8oz piece beef fillet or
  thick sirloin steak
1 tsp sunflower oil
2 tbsp Thai fish sauce
juice of 1 lime
1 tsp soft, dark-brown sugar
1 small clove garlic, chopped
1 shallot, peeled and finely
  chopped
2 tbsp fresh cilantro,
  chopped
1 Thai chile pepper, thinly
  sliced
½ package mixed salad
  leaves

Ingredients for 4

4oz rice noodles
2 tbsp crushed Szechwan
  peppercorns
1lb piece beef fillet or
  thick sirloin steak
1 tbsp sunflower oil
4 tbsp Thai fish sauce
juice of 2 limes
2 tsp soft, dark-brown sugar
1 large clove garlic, chopped
2 shallots, peeled and finely
  chopped
4 tbsp fresh cilantro,
  chopped
2 Thai chile peppers, thinly
  sliced
1 packaget mixed salad
  leaves

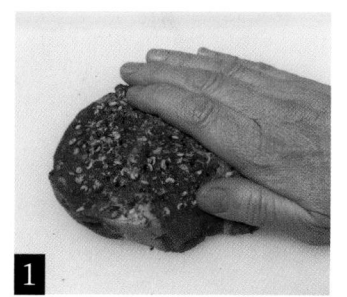

1 Cook the rice noodles in boiling water according to the package instructions, drain, and refresh under cold running water. Rub the steak all over with the peppercorns and press on to coat the meat. If you want to prepare this dish ahead of time, keep the cooked noodles and peppered steak chilled until needed. Heat the oil in a nonstick skillet.

2 Place the beef in the skillet and cook over a high heat for 2 minutes each side, turning once, until seared and browned all over. Place the steak in a warmed dish, cover with aluminum foil, and leave to rest for 5 minutes. Leaving the meat to rest will make it become more tender and easy to carve thinly.

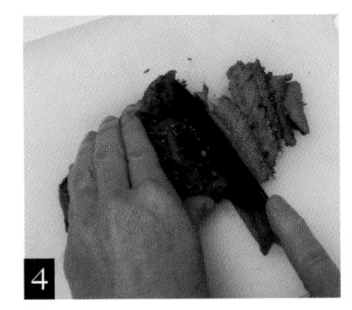

3 Mix the fish sauce, lime juice, and sugar together in a glass pitcher or jar, then stir in the garlic, shallot, chile pepper, and cilantro. Whisk together with a fork or put on the lid and shake the jar well.

4 Place the meat on a chopping board and slice the beef as thinly as possible into strips with a sharp knife or cleaver. Place the noodles and salad leaves on a serving dish, add the beef strips and toss together with the dressing. Serve warm or cold.

Sautéed Chile Chicken Breasts

spicy

I love the flavor of fresh herbs, and usually grow my own, but the fresh herb and spice pastes now sold in tubes are handy for adding zest to dishes in the winter, when fresh herbs are scarce.

Ingredients for 2

1¾ tbsp butter, softened
2 tsp fresh red-chile paste
2 tsp fresh cilantro paste
1 clove garlic, peeled and chopped
½ tsp ground cumin
finely grated zest of ½ lemon
2 chicken breasts
1 tbsp olive oil
salt
black pepper, freshly ground

Ingredients for 4

¼ cup butter, softened
1 tbsp fresh red-chile paste
4 tbsp fresh cilantro paste
2 cloves garlic, peeled and chopped
1 tsp ground cumin
finely grated zest of 1 lemon
4 chicken breasts
2 tbsp olive oil
salt
black pepper, freshly ground

5 minutes preparation
5 minutes freezing
12 minutes cooking

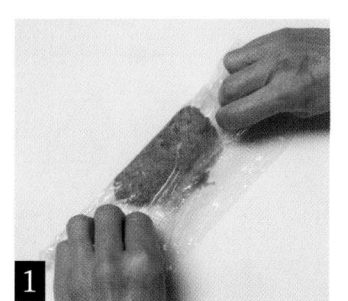

1 Place the butter in a bowl and beat together with the chile and cilantro pastes and the garlic, cumin, and lemon zest. Place on a piece of plastic wrap, shape into a sausage shape, and freeze for 5 minutes to firm. If you want to prepare ahead, make the flavored butter and keep it wrapped in aluminum foil in the freezer until you need it.

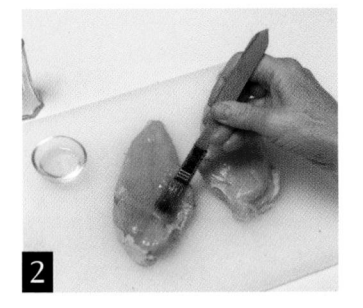

2 Heat a nonstick griddle pan or a broiler to hot. Brush the chicken breasts all over with the oil and season with salt and freshly ground black pepper.

3 Place the oiled chicken breasts on a griddle or broiler pan and sauté or broil for 6 minutes on each side, until browned and tender. Turn the chicken over regularly during the cooking time with kitchen tongs.

4 Place each chicken breast on a hot serving plate. Place the chilled or frozen butter on a chopping board and cut into 2 (4) slices with a very sharp knife. Position 1 portion of spiced butter centrally on top of each chicken piece. Serve with thick ribbon noodles and a crisp arugula salad, or stir-fry Chinese vegetables.

Pork With Prunes

Pork fillets are so easy to cook, and they need hardly any preparation. With no fiddly bones or skin, they are also easy to carve.

Ingredients for 2

8 pitted prunes
²/₃ cup red or white wine
2 x 6oz pork tenderloin fillets
1 tbsp all-purpose flour
salt
black pepper, freshly ground
1 tbsp butter
1 tbsp red-currant jelly
½ tsp Worcestershire sauce
4 tbsp heavy cream

Ingredients for 4

16 pitted prunes
1¼ cups red or white wine
4 x 6oz pork tenderloin fillets
2 tbsp all-purpose flour
salt
black pepper, freshly ground
2 tbsps butter
2 tbsp red-currant jelly
1 tsp Worcestershire sauce
8 tbsp heavy cream

5 minutes preparation
12 minutes cooking

1 Place the prunes in the wine and heat to just below boiling in a small pan or in the microwave oven. Leave the prunes to soak and become plump while you cook the other ingredients.

2 Dab any moisture from the pork fillets with paper towels. Spread the flour out onto a plate and season with salt and freshly ground black pepper. Roll the fillets in flour to coat them all over lightly.

3 Heat the butter in a heavy-based nonstick skillet and fry the fillets on all sides for 5 minutes, until browned all over. Add the prunes and wine, the red-currant jelly, and Worcestershire sauce, stir, then simmer for 5 minutes.

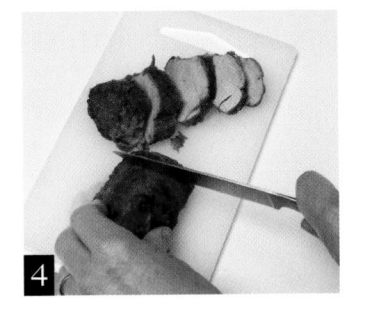

4 Remove the fillets from the sauce, place on a board, and slice thickly. Add the cream to the skillet and cook for a further 2 minutes, stirring constantly. Pour the sauce over the slices and serve with mashed potatoes and your choice of green vegetables.

Shrimp & Vegetable Risotto

Family Favorite

There is nothing simpler to prepare than a rice dish—this one is cooked all in one pan to make an easy supper dish.

Ingredients for 2

- 1 tbsp sunflower oil
- 1 small onion, finely chopped
- 1 small clove garlic, peeled and chopped
- ½ cup arborio or risotto rice
- ¼ tsp saffron threads
- finely grated zest of ½ lemon
- 2 cups hot fish stock
- ½ cup snow peas
- ¼ cup baby zucchini, sliced
- ½ cup large shrimp, cooked and peeled
- 2 tbsp fresh Italian parsley, chopped

Ingredients for 4

- 2 tbsp sunflower oil
- 1 onion, finely chopped
- 1 large clove garlic, peeled and chopped
- 1 cup arborio or risotto rice
- ¼ tsp saffron threads
- finely grated zest of 1 lemon
- 3 cups hot fish stock
- 1 cup snow peas
- ½ cup baby zucchini, sliced
- 1 cup large shrimp, cooked and peeled
- 2 tbsp fresh Italian parsley, chopped

5 minutes preparation
25 minutes cooking

1 Heat the oil in a large, heavy-based, deep skillet and fry the onion and garlic for 2 minutes to soften. Add the rice and saffron and stir together over a medium heat to coat the grains of rice. Continue to stir the rice for about 1 minute.

2 Add the lemon zest and a quarter of the hot fish stock. Stir well and simmer for 5 minutes, until the rice has absorbed the stock. Stir to prevent the rice from sticking to the base of the skillet.

3 Repeat with another quarter of the hot stock and cook until the liquid is absorbed. Add the snow peas, zucchini, and another quarter of the stock and cook for 5

minutes until the stock is completely absorbed.

4 Add the remaining stock and cook for a further 5 minutes. About 2 minutes before the end of cooking time, stir in the shrimp to heat through. Don't be tempted to overcook them, as they will become tough. Serve sprinkled with fresh, chopped parsley.

Thai Fish Cakes

Family Favorite

You'll need a small food processor to make this dish. These machines are a great investment, and certainly save on time and dish-washing.

Ingredients for 2

2oz fresh white bread,
crusts removed
9oz cod, skin and
bones removed
½ chile pepper, deseeded
and chopped
1in-piece fresh ginger root,
peeled and finely
chopped
1 tbsp fresh cilantro,
chopped
2 tsp fish sauce
1 egg white
salt
1 tbsp sunflower oil
mixed salad leaves
chile dipping sauce

Ingredients for 4

4oz fresh white bread,
crusts removed
1lb 2oz cod, skin and
bones removed
1 chile pepper, deseeded
and chopped
2in-piece fresh ginger root,
peeled and finely
chopped
2 tbsp fresh cilantro,
chopped
1 tbsp fish sauce
2 egg whites
salt
2 tbsp sunflower oil
mixed salad leaves
chile dipping sauce

10 minutes preparation

6 minutes cooking

1 Place the bread in a food processor and process into fine crumbs.

2 Chop the cod into chunks and remove any fine bones. Add the fish to the processor with the breadcrumbs, chile pepper, ginger, cilantro, fish sauce, and egg white. Then season with a little salt.

3 Process the mixture until blended and smooth. Divide into 4 (8) pieces and shape into patties.

4 Heat the oil in a large nonstick skillet and fry the cakes for 3 minutes on each side, until golden brown. Pat with paper towels and serve with the salad leaves and dipping sauce.

Pasta With Crab

Pantry Special

I always keep a can of canned crab in my pantry—it's handy for an instant appetizer with fresh avocados, or add it to hot pasta with a cream or a tomato sauce.

Ingredients for 2

1 cup bowtie pasta
1 tbsp olive oil
½ red chile pepper, deseeded and sliced
1 clove garlic, peeled and crushed
1in-piece fresh ginger root, peeled and chopped
¾ cup tomato passata sauce
6oz can canned white crab
½ lemon

Ingredients for 4

2 cups bowtie pasta
2 tbsp olive oil
1 red chile pepper, deseeded and sliced
2 cloves garlic, peeled and crushed
1in-piece fresh ginger root, peeled and chopped
1¾ cups tomato passata sauce
2 x 6oz cans canned white crab
1 lemon

10 minutes preparation
12 minutes cooking

1 Place a a large pan of salted water on to boil and cook the pasta according to the packge instructions. Drain and keep warm.

2 Meanwhile, heat the oil in a large skillet and fry the chile pepper, garlic, and ginger for 5 minutes over a low heat until softened.

3 Add the passata and cook for 5 minutes. Add the crab and cook for 2 minutes to warm through.

4 Slice the zest from the lemon in thin strips. Add the sauce to the cooked pasta and toss together. Serve sprinkled with the lemon strips.

Trout Fillets With Shallot Butter

Family Favorite

Fresh trout fillets blend with a tangy shallot butter for a real treat. If you can't find fresh trout, use skinned salmon fillets instead.

12 minutes preparation

20 minutes cooking

Ingredients for 2

**12oz old potatoes,
peeled**
2 tbsp light cream
2¾ tbsp butter
1 tbsp all-purpose flour
salt
white pepper, freshly ground
**2 x 7oz trout fillets,
    skin removed**
1 tsp sunflower oil
**2 shallots, peeled and finely
    chopped**
3 tbsp white- wine vinegar
**1 tbsp fresh chives,
    chopped**

Ingredients for 4

**1½lb old potatoes,
peeled**
4 tbsp light cream
½ cup butter
2 tbsp all-purpose flour
salt
white pepper, freshly ground
**4 x 7oz trout fillets,
    skin removed**
2 tsp sunflower oil
**4 shallots, peeled and finely
    chopped**
6 tbsp white-wine vinegar
**2 tbsp fresh chives,
    chopped**

1 Boil the potatoes until tender, then drain and mash with the cream and 1 tbsp (1¼ tbsps) butter. Meanwhile, spread the flour on a plate and season with salt and ground white pepper. Dust the fillets in the flour to coat.

2 Heat half the remaining butter in a large nonstick skillet with the oil and fry the trout for 3–4 minutes on each side until golden. Remove to a plate and keep warm.

3 Heat the remaining butter in the skillet and fry the shallots for 2–3 minutes until softened. Add the vinegar and cook for 3 minutes, until the liquid reduces slightly.

4 Spoon the shallot butter over the fish and sprinkle with the chopped chives. Serve with the mashed potato.

Monkfish With Oyster Sauce

Low Fat

Monkfish has a delicate flavor and a firm textur,e making it ideal for kabobs. Look for monkfish tails, often sold more cheaply by fish suppliers.

Ingredients for 2

10oz monkfish tail fillets,
   skinned and boned
⅓ cup Chinese oyster
   sauce
1 tbsp unsalted butter
2 tbsp white wine
2 green onions, finely
   shredded
a few fresh cilantro sprigs

Ingredients for 4

1¼lb monkfish tail fillets,
   skinned and boned
⅔ cup Chinese oyster
   sauce
1¾ tbsp unsalted butter
4 tbsp white wine
4 green onions, finely
   shredded
a few fresh cilantro sprigs

10 minutes preparation

15 minutes cooking

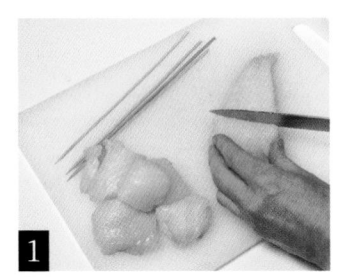

1 Cut the monkfish into 1in cubes and thread on to short, wooden skewers.

2 Put a plate or steamer basket in the base of a steaming pan and place the fish skewers on this. Cover the steaming pan with a lid or a sheet of aluminum foil. Steam the fish over a medium heat for 15 minutes, until it is tender.

3 Meanwhile, gently heat the oyster sauce with the butter and white wine in a small saucepan.

4 Drizzle the sauce over the fish and serve sprinkled with the green onions and cilantro. Accompany the fish with plain, boiled rice and stir-fried bok choy.

Sautéed Sea Bass With Herbs

Superquick

You'll find sea bass on the menu in Mediterranean restaurants, but you'll also see it on sale at your local fish suppliers. It's very simple to sauté, so make the most of this delicacy.

Ingredients for 2

2 tsp black-olive tapenade
2 x 5oz sea bass fillets
1 tbsp olive oil
/4oz ripe tomatoes
1 tbsp fresh parsley
1 tbsp fresh basil
juice of ½ lime

Ingredients for 4

4 tsp black-olive tapenade
4 x 5oz sea bass fillets
2 tbsp olive oil
8oz ripe tomatoes
2 tbsp fresh parsley
2 tbsp fresh basil
juice of 1 lime

5 minutes preparation
10 minutes cooking

1 Spread the olive tapenade thinly on the fleshy side of the fish. Heat half of the oil in a nonstick skillet and cook the fish, skin-side down, for 4 minutes.

2 Turn the fish over and cook the fillets for a further 3–4 minutes until the fish is cooked. Remove to warmed serving plates and keep warm.

3 Meanwhile, cut the tomatoes in half, scoop out the seeds, and chop the flesh into small dice. Chop the herbs roughly and combine with the tomatoes.

4 Heat the remaining oil in the skillet and lightly sauté the tomato mixture for 1 minute. Add the lime juice and cook for 1 further minute, then serve sprinkled over the fillets.

Pesto-broiled Lamb Chops

Easy Entertaining

The Italian pesto sauce that coats these lamb chops keeps them tender during broiling and adds a delicious, herby tang.

Ingredients for 2

- 1 tbsp olive oil
- 2 shallots, peeled and finely chopped
- 1 clove garlic, peeled and chopped
- ½ cup baby eggplant, diced
- ½ cup baby zucchini, diced
- 7oz can diced tomatoes
- 1 tbsp red wine
- ½ tsp dried oregano
- 4 small lamb loin chops
- 2 tbsp green-pesto sauce

Ingredients for 4

- 2 tbsp olive oil
- 4 shallots, peeled and finely chopped
- 2 cloves garlic, peeled and chopped
- 1¼ cups baby eggplant, diced
- 1¼ cups baby zucchini, diced
- 14oz can diced tomatoes
- 2 tbsp red wine
- 1 tsp dried oregano
- 8 small lamb loin chops
- 4 tbsp green-pesto sauce

10 minutes preparation

10 minutes cooking

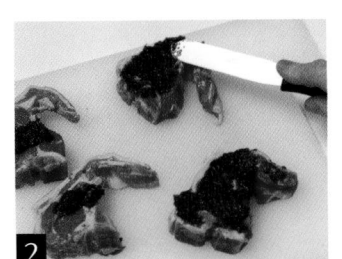

1 Heat the oil in a large pan and fry the shallots and garlic for 1 minute to soften. Add the diced eggplant and zucchini and stir-fry for 2 minutes. Add the tomatoes, wine, and oregano, cover, and simmer for 10 minutes.

2 Preheat the broiler to high. Spread both sides of the chops with pesto sauce.

3 Broil the lamb chops for 5 minutes on each side, then place on a warmed serving plate to keep warm, and rest for 5 minutes.

4 Serve the chops with ratatouille and chunks of crusty bread.

Steak With Herby Cheese Sauce

Quick and Easy

Crispy sautéed potatoes usually take ages to cook, so try this easy way with small, new potatoes instead.

5 minutes preparation
15 minutes cooking

Ingredients for 2

10oz small, new potatoes in their skins, scrubbed
2 tsp olive oil, plus a little extra
2 x 6oz beef sirloin or rump steaks
black pepper, freshly ground
¼ cup garlic and herb cream cheese
3 tbsp milk

Ingredients for 4

1¼lb small, new potatoes in their skins, scrubbed
4 tsp olive oil, plus a little extra
4 x /6oz beef sirloin or rump steaks
black pepper, freshly ground
½ cup garlic and herb cream cheese
6 tbsp milk

1 Boil the new potatoes for 10 minutes until half-cooked, then drain well and cut in half. Heat the oil in a large nonstick skillet and fry the potatoes on all sides until golden, for 5 minutes.

2 Preheat the broiler to high. Rub the steak all over with a little olive oil, then season with black pepper. When the broiler is hot, cook the meat for 3 to 4 minutes on each side, or a little less if you prefer to eat the steak rare. Keep warm on a plate to rest for 5 minutes before serving.

3 Place the cheese in a small saucepan with the milk and heat gently until melted together.

4 Serve the steak with the potatoes, with the garlic and herb sauce drizzled over.

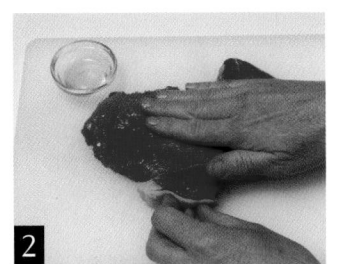

Lamb Kabobs

Easy Entertaining

These easy kabobs are ideal to cook over the barbecue grill. If you prepare them ahead, you can leave them in the marinade to make them even more tender.

Ingredients for 2

12oz boneless leg of lamb
½ green bell pepper
2 red onions, peeled
4 bay leaves, halved

Marinade

1 tbsp olive oil
1 clove garlic, crushed
1 tbsp dried oregano
juice of ½ lemon

Ingredients for 4

1½lb boneless leg of lamb
1 green bell pepper
4 red onions, peeled
8 bay leaves, halved

Marinade

2 tbsp olive oil
2 cloves garlic, crushed
2 tbsp dried oregano
juice of 1 lemon

10 minutes preparation
10 minutes chilling
10 minutes cooking

1 Trim any extra fat from the meat and cut into 1in cubes. Halve the bell pepper, remove the seeds, and cut into 1in dice. Peel the onion and cut into thick slices 1in wide.

2 Place the meat, bell pepper, onions, and bay leaves in a shallow dish. Mix the oil, garlic, oregano, and lemon juice together and sprinkle into the dish. Chill for 15 minutes (or longer if there is time).

3 Preheat the broiler or a grill to hot. Thread the meat, peppers, onions, and bay leaves alternately on to metal skewers.

4 Broil under a high heat for 4 minutes, then turn down the heat and broil for a further 6 minutes, until the lamb is cooked through and tender. Serve with warmed pita breads and accompanied by a green salad with tomatoes, olives, and feta cheese.

Lamb Kidneys With Mushrooms

Family Favorite

Keep some lamb kidneys handy in the freezer, and you can always rustle up this quick, savory supper

Ingredients for 2

- 3 lamb kidneys, thawed if frozen
- 1¾ tbsp butter
- 1¾ tbsp lard leaves
- 4 boiling onions, peeled
- ½ cup white mushrooms, halved
- ½ tbsp all-purpose flour
- 5 tbsp hot beef stock
- 5 tbsp red wine
- ½ tbsp tomato paste
- 1 tsp Worcestershire sauce

Ingredients for 4

- 6 lamb kidneys, thawed if frozen
- ¼ cup butter
- ¼ cup lard leaves
- 8 boiling onions, peeled
- 1 cup white mushrooms, halved
- 1 tbsp all-purpose flour
- ⅔ cup hot beef stock
- ⅔ cup red wine
- 1 tbsp tomato paste
- 2 tsp Worcestershire sauce

10 minutes preparation

15 minutes cooking

1 Remove the skin from the kidneys, cut them in half, and snip out the white core in the center with kitchen scissors. Cut each half into 3 pieces.

2 Heat the butter and fry the lard leaves for 2 minutes, until the fat runs. Add the onions and stir-fry for 2 minutes, until browned.

3 Add the mushrooms and kidney pieces and then stir-fry for 3 minutes. Now add the flour and mix to make a sandy texture.

4 Add the stock, wine, tomato paste, and Worcestershire sauce and bring to the boil. Turn down the heat to a simmer, and cook, covered, for 5 minutes, stirring occasionally. Serve with tagliatelle or ribbon noodles.

Shrimp & Lemon Ribbons

Easy Entertaining

This is a great recipe for using ripe, home-grown, fresh tomatoes in the summer months.

5 minutes preparation
15 minutes cooking

Ingredients for 2

7oz pappardelle or
   tagliatelle pasta
2 tsp olive oil
1 small clove garlic, chopped
3 ripe, medium-sized
   tomatoes
finely grated zest of ½ lemon
¼ tsp dried red-pepper flakes
¾ cup cooked, peeled
   large shrimp
salt
black pepper, freshly ground
1 tbsp fresh Italian parsley,
   chopped

Ingredients for 4

14oz pappardelle or
   tagliatelle pasta
4 tsp olive oil
1 large clove garlic, chopped
6 ripe, medium-sized
   tomatoes
finely grated zest of 1 lemon
½ tsp dried red-pepper flakes
1½ cups cooked, peeled
   large shrimp
salt
black pepper, freshly ground
2 tbsp fresh flat leaf parsley,
   chopped

1 Heat a large pan of salted water and put the pasta on to cook for about 10 minutes, or according to the package instructions.

2 Heat the oil in a large, deep saucepan and fry the garlic for about 1 minute to soften. Chop the tomatoes finely, add to the pan, and simmer for about 6 minutes, until they become soft and pulpy.

3 Add the lemon zest, red-pepper flakes, and shrimp to the pan and cook for about 2 minutes, until heated through. Season with salt and black pepper.

4 Drain the pasta well and place it back in the cooking pan. Add the sauce with the parsley and toss together to mix, then divide between warmed bowls before serving.

Desserts

Broiled Pineapple With Caramel Cream

Quick and Easy

This easy dessert is great for barbecues. If you have a clean grill rack handy, you can cook the carameliszd slices over the hot coals.

10 minutes preparation
5 minutes cooking

Ingredients for 2

- **²/₃ cup sour cream**
- **1 vanilla bean**
- **1 tbsp ready-made toffee-fudge sauce**
- **½ fresh pineapple**
- **3 tbsp confectioner's sugar**

Ingredients for 4

- **1¼ cups sour cream**
- **2 vanilla beans**
- **2 tbsp ready-made toffee-fudge sauce**
- **1 fresh pineapple**
- **6 tbsp confectioner's sugar**

1 Preheat the broiler. Place the sour cream into a small bowl. Scoop the seeds from the vanilla bean(s) and stir into the sour cream. Dot small spoonfuls of the toffee sauce over the cream and chill until needed.

2 Cut the green top and the base from the pineapple and place the pineapple on a board. Cut the skin away in wide strips from the top to the base.

3 Cut out the woody "eyes" all round the pineapple, then slice the fruit thinly.

4 Dust each slice with confectioner's sugar and place on a broiler or grill pan. Broil for 1 minute on each side, then serve immediately with the prepared caramel cream.

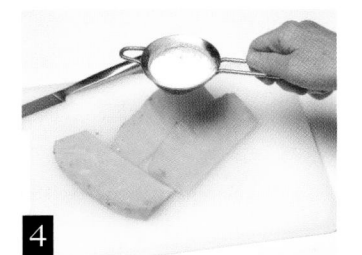

Cook's Tip:

If a pineapple is fresh and ready to eat, it will have a sweet, ripe smell.

Banana Splits With Chocolate Sauce

Family Favorite

Get the kids involved and let them help to create these special treats.

Ingredients for 2

4oz dark chocolate
1 tbsp butter
½ tbsp maple syrup
2 ripe bananas
⅔ cup whipping cream
1 tbsp confectioner's sugar
½ tsp vanilla extract
2 tbsp ready-made toffee-fudge sauce
1 tbsp mixed, chopped nuts

Ingredients for 4

7oz dark chocolate
1¾ tsps butter
1 tbsp maple syrup
4 ripe bananas
1¼ cups whipping cream
2 tbsp confectioner's sugar
1 tsp vanilla extract
4 tbsp ready-made toffee-fudge sauce
2 tbsp mixed, chopped nuts

10 minutes preparation
4 minutes cooking

1 Break the chocolate into squares and place in a heatproof or microwave-proof bowl with the butter and syrup. Heat over a pan of simmering water, or in the microwave on low, until melted.

2 Peel the bananas and cut them in half lengthwise. Whip the cream until it forms soft peaks, then fold in the confectioner's sugar and the vanilla extract.

3 Pipe or spoon the cream down the middle of each banana, press the two halves back together, and place each on a plate.

4 Spoon a tablespoon of toffee-fudge sauce over each banana, then drizzle each one with chocolate sauce. Sprinkle with nuts and serve immediately.

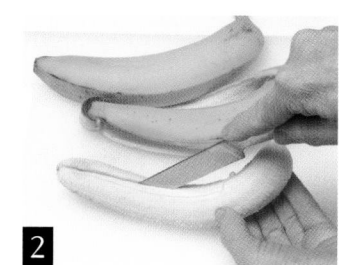

Tropical Trifle

Easy Entertaining

Serve this easy-to-make trifle after a special Sunday lunch, and worry about the calories later!

Ingredients for 2

4oz ready-made ginger cake
8oz can pineapple rings
   in juice
1 tbsp dark rum
1 small mango, peeled and
   chopped
1¼ cups whipping cream
3oz carton dairy custard
   sauce

Ingredients for 4

8oz ready-made ginger cake
1lb can pineapple rings
   in juice
2 tbsp dark rum
1 large mango, peeled and
   chopped
2½ cups whipping cream
5oz carton dairy custard
   sauce

20 minutes preparation

No cooking

1 Cut the ginger cake into thick slices to fit into the base of a glass dish. Sprinkle with the rum and 2 (4) tablespoons of juice from the tin of pineapple.

2 Reserve a quarter of the pineapple rings, then chop the remainder and mix with the fresh mangoes. Place over the cake layer.

3 Whip the cream until it forms soft peaks. Fold half the cream together with the custard sauce and spread over the fruit.

4 Spoon the remaining cream into a pastry bag fitted with a star nozzle and pipe a lattice or border over the top of the custard. Cut the remaining pineapple into neat pieces and decorate the top of the trifle. Chill until needed.

Microwave Chocolate Pudding

Family Favorite

This old-fashioned pudding takes ages to cook in a steaming pan, but you can cook it in minutes in the microwave oven.

Ingredients for 2

1¾ tbsp cocoa powder
½ cup self-rising flour
½ tsp baking powder
½ cup soft margarine
½ cup soft, dark-brown sugar
2 tbsp milk
2 eggs

Custard sauce

2 tbsp custard powder or instant vanilla-pudding mix
1 tbsp granulated sugar
2½ cups whole milk

10 minutes preparation

6 minutes cooking
(in a 650-watt microwave oven)

1 Grease a 4-cup-capacity microwave-proof pudding bowl. Sift the cocoa, flour, and baking powder into a bowl.

2 Add the margarine, sugar, milk, and eggs and beat until smooth. Spoon into the bowl and cover with plastic wrap. Make a ¼in pleat in the plastic wrap and pierce to let the pudding rise.

3 Cook on high for 6 minutes, turning the bowl halfway through cooking. Loosen the plastic wrap and stand for 5 minutes.

4 In a large microwave-proof pitcher, blend the custard powder or pudding mix and sugar with 3 tablespoons of milk until smooth. Add the remaining milk and cook on high for 5 minutes, stirring halfway through.

Cook's Tip:

It is important to leave the pudding to stand and settle for 5 minutes before serving it. Don't turn it out of its bowl straight away as it will be far too hot to serve and could cause a burn.

Mangoes With Marsala Cream

Family Favorite

You'll find that pomegranates are usually only available in the winter months, but they do add a wonderful splash of color. This is a great alternative dessert for Christmas, if your guests don't want a traditional, heavy pudding.

Ingredients for 2

- **1 ripe mango**
- **1 papaya**
- **1 pomegranate, halved**
- **⅔ cup heavy cream**
- **2 tbsp Marsala or sweet sherry**
- **1 tbsp confectioner's sugar**
- **4 biscotti**

Ingredients for 4

- **2 ripe mangoes**
- **2 papayas**
- **2 pomegranates, halved**
- **1¼ cups heavy cream**
- **3 tbsp Marsala or sweet sherry**
- **3 tbsp confectioner's sugar**
- **8 biscotti**

15 minutes preparation
No cooking

1 Peel and remove the pit from the mango and cut the flesh into thin slices. Peel the papaya, cut in half, scoop out the seeds, and cut the flesh into slices.

2 Arrange the fruit on a plate. Scoop out the seeds from the pomegranate and sprinkle over the slices.

3 Whip the cream until it forms soft peaks. Fold in the Marsala or sherry and the confectioner's sugar. (If you want to prepare the dish ahead of time, then chill for 1 hour at this stage.)

4 Add a few spoons of the cream to each plate and serve with the biscotti.

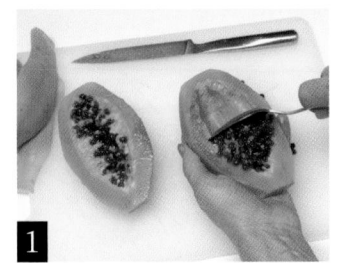

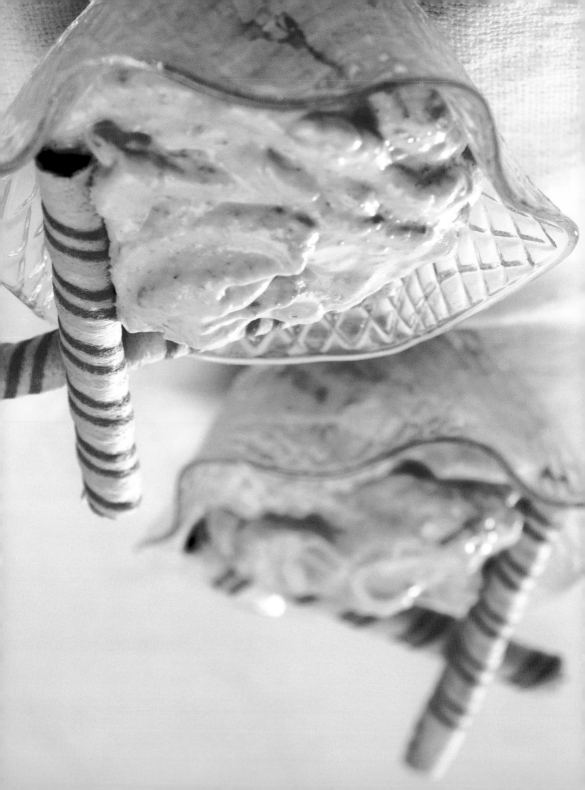

Raspberry Fluff

Quick and Easy

I always make the most of luscious, soft summer fruits when they are cheap and plentiful. This dessert has the lovely, fresh tang of berry fruits mixed with a light, creamy foam.

Ingredients for 2

½ cup fresh or frozen raspberries
3oz can evaporated milk, chilled
1 tbsp superfine sugar
½ cup thick Greek yogurt
4 wafer-roll cookies or ladyfingers
2 fresh mint sprigs

Ingredients for 4

1 cup fresh or frozen raspberries
6oz can evaporated milk, chilled
1 tbsp superfine sugar
¾ cup thick Greek yogurt
8 wafer-roll cookies or ladyfingers
4 fresh mint sprigs

12 minutes preparation
No cooking

1 Place the berries in a small food processor and blend to a paste. Push through a sieve to remove the pips.

2 Whisk the evaporated milk until doubled in volume, then whisk in the sugar.

3 Fold in the fruit paste, then fold in the thick yoghurt.

4 Spoon into individual serving glasses and serve each one with two wafer-roll cookies or ladyfingers and a sprig of mint.

Cook's Tip:

If you don't have raspberries, you could use fresh strawberries or fresh or frozen blackberries in the same way.

Fruity Toasts

Family Favorite

If you have any leftover pannetone from Christmas, you'll find that it is delicious toasted, but raisin or fruit bread, or good-quality fruit buns, split and toasted, are just as good.

Ingredients for 2

¼ cup fresh strawberries
¼ cup fresh raspberries
¼ cup fresh blackberries
2 heaped tbsp seedless
   raspberry preserves
1 tbsp lemon juice
2 x 2oz slices pannetone,
raisin or fruit bread,
   or fruit buns
4 tbsp clotted cream or
   whipped heavy cream

Ingredients for 4

½ cup fresh strawberries
½ cup fresh raspberries
½ cup fresh blackberries
4 heaped tbsp seedless
   raspberry preserves
2 tbsp lemon juice
4 x 2oz slices pannetone,
raisin or fruit bread,
   or fruit buns
8 tbsp clotted cream or
   whipped heavy cream

15 minutes preparation
5 minutes cooking

1 Trim any stalks and leaves from the fruit and slice the strawberries if they are large.

2 Place the fruit in a bowl then warm the preserves together with the lemon juice until melted. Pour over the fruit and toss together.

3 Toast the pannetone or fruit-bread slices or buns on both sides and place on serving plates.

4 Divide the fruit into 2 (4) portions and pile up on each toasted slice. Top each with 2 spoons of cream and serve immediately.

Cook's Tip:

You could replace the fresh strawberries, raspberries and blackberries with ¾ cup (1½ cups) partly thawed, frozen mixed berries and cherries.

Banoffi Ice Cream Sundaes

Family Favorite

If the family need cheering up, make them this special treat from handy ingredients in the freezer and pantry.

Ingredients for 2

1¼ cups vanilla ice cream
¼ cup vanilla fudge
1 ripe banana
2 tbsp ready-made toffee-
  fudge sauce
4 wafer-roll cookies
1 bar of flaked chocolate

Ingredients for 4

2½ cups vanilla ice cream
½ cup vanilla fudge
2 ripe bananas
4 tbsp ready-made toffee-
  fudge sauce
8 wafer-roll cookies
2 bars of flaked chocolate

8 minutes preparation

No cooking

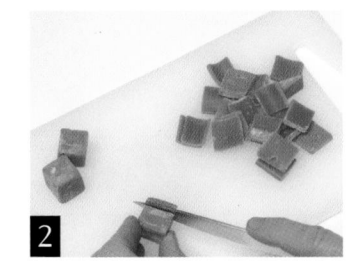

1 Place 2 (4) scoops of ice cream in the bases of glass serving dishes.

2 Chop the fudge into thin slices and scatter over the ice cream. Peel and slice the bananas and scatter over the fudge.

3 Add another scoop of ice cream and drizzle with toffee-fudge sauce.

4 Place wafer-roll cookies in each glass and sprinkle the top with chocolate flakes. Serve immediately.

Cook's Tip:

Use good-quality, block ice cream for this dessert. The soft-scoop ice cream that is sold in plastic containers will not form firm scoops, and will start to melt more quickly than block ice cream.

Rhubarb & Orange Pots

Family Favorite

Fresh rhubarb is delicious combined with orange in these creamy little desserts.

Ingredients for 2

8oz fresh, pink rhubarb, chopped
1¾ tbsp butter
finely grated zest and juice of ½ orange, plus some thin strips of zest
1¾ tbsp superfine sugar
⅔ cup heavy cream

Ingredients for 4

1lb fresh, pink rhubarb, chopped
¼ cup butter
finely grated zest and juice of 1 orange, plus some thin strips of zest
¼ cup superfine sugar
1¼ cups heavy cream

20 minutes preparation
20 minutes cooking

1

2

3

1 Place the rhubarb in a pan with the butter, orange rind, and juice and 1 (2) tablespoon(s) of water.

2 Cover and simmer gently for 8 minutes, until the rhubarb is soft. Stir in the sugar and taste the fruit: if it is too sharp, add more sugar. Place in a bowl to cool.

3 Whip the cream until thick and fold into the cold fruit. Spoon into 2 (4) small serving dishes or glasses and chill for 20 minutes.

4 Just before serving, sprinkle with thin strips of orange zest.

Cook's Tip:

If you don't have rhubarb to hand, you could use 1lb fresh, ripe gooseberries instead.

Chocolate Custard Bananas

 *Quick and Easy*

Round off a family meal with this quick and easy treat, popular with both adults and children alike.

Ingredients for 2

- **1 tbsp custard powder or instant vanilla-pudding mix**
- **1 tbsp superfine sugar**
- **1¼ cups whole milk**
- **4oz milk chocolate**
- **2 ripe bananas**

Ingredients for 4

- **2 tbsp custard powder or instant vanilla-pudding mix**
- **2 tbsp superfine sugar**
- **2½ cups whole milk**
- **8oz milk chocolate**
- **4 ripe bananas**

5 minutes preparation
10 minutes cooking

1 Mix the custard powder or pudding-mix, sugar, and 2 (4) tablespoons of milk into a smooth paste.

2 Heat the remaining milk to just below boiling. Pour over the custard paste and mix well, off the heat.

3 Return the pan to the heat and stir until thick and smooth. Break the chocolate into squares and whisk into the hot custard until smooth and completely melted.

4 Peel and slice the bananas and stir into the custard. Serve immediately.

Cook's Tip:

If you don't have any bananas, use drained, canned peach slices or apricot halves instead.

Strawberries With Mascarpone

Easy Entertaining

This dessert makes the most of luscious summer fruits. To make life simple, you can marinade the strawberries ahead of time.

Ingredients for 2

- **8oz fresh, ripe strawberries**
- **2 tbsp amaretto or peach liqueur**
- **2 tbsp superfine sugar**
- **½ the white of 1 large egg**
- **¼ cup mascarpone cheese**
- **cocoa powder**

Ingredients for 4

- **1lb fresh, ripe strawberries**
- **4 tbsp amaretto or peach liqueur**
- **4 tbsp superfine sugar**
- **the white of 1 large egg**
- **½ cup mascarpone cheese**
- **cocoa powder**

10 minutes preparation

No cooking

1

1 Remove the hulls from the strawberries and toss in the liqueur with half of the sugar. Chill for 10 minutes.

2 Whisk the egg white to soft peaks, add the remaining sugar, and whisk again to form floppy peaks.

3 Fold a spoonful of the egg white into the cheese to slacken it, then fold in the remaining egg white gently.

4 Divide the strawberries and their juices between glass serving dishes. Top each with the mascarpone cream and then sprinkle with some cocoa powder.

2

3

Caramelized Oranges

No Fat

This simple dessert is particularly good served at the end of a rich meal. It is easy to make ahead and chill, which means you can serve it straight from the fridge.

Ingredients for 2

3 large navel oranges
½ cup golden granulated
sugar
⅔ cup water

Ingredients for 4

6 large navel oranges
1 cup golden granulated
sugar
1 cup water

1 Using a vegetable peeler, peel the outside rind from 1 (2) of the oranges. Cut the rind into very fine strips.

2 Cut the skin and pith from all of the remaining oranges and cut the flesh into thin slices. Arrange the orange slices in a heatproof serving dish and scatter the strips over the top.

3 Place the sugar with half of the water in a heavy-based

saucepan and heat gently until every grain of sugar has dissolved. Heat the pan, without stirring, until the sugar turns to a deep caramel.

4 Remove the pan from the heat and, standing clear to avoid any spitting, carefully add the remaining water. Stir to dissolve, then pour over the oranges slices in the dish. Chill for 15 minutes or longer, then serve with thick cream or Greek yogurt.

Cook's Tip:

Look out for navel oranges during the winter months. They are large, sweet oranges with lots of juicy flesh, but no pits.

Lemon & Kiwi-fruit Layers

Family Favorite

Bright-green kiwi fruits make this creamy lemon dessert light and refreshing.

Ingredients for 2

2 kiwi fruits
6 amaretti cookies
2/3 cup whipping cream
3 tbsp sweet white wine
2 tbsp lemon conserve

Ingredients for 4

4 kiwi fruits
12 amaretti cookies
3/4 cup whipping cream
5 tbsp sweet white wine
4 tbsp lemon conserve

10 minutes preparation

No cooking

1 Peel the kiwi fruit and slice thinly. Now crush the cookies roughly, then place them in the bases of 2 (4) glass serving dishes.

2 Place the cream, wine, and lemon conserve in a bowl and whisk until the mixture forms soft peaks.

3 Spoon a layer of cream over the cookies, add a layer of kiwis, reserving a few slices for decoration.

4 Top with the remaining cream, then decorate with kiwi slices. Serve immediately as the creamy mixture will eventually separate.

Cook's Tip:

Instead of kiwis, you could use any tart, fresh fruits. Try 1 cup peeled and sliced, fresh (or canned) apricots, peaches, or nectarines, or fresh, sliced strawberries.

Cherry Pancakes

Family Favorite

Make these pancakes ahead of time, then you can whip up this dessert in just minutes.

Ingredients for 2

¼ cup all-purpose flour
½ egg, beaten
⅔ cup reduced-fat milk
½ tbsp sunflower oil, plus
    a little extra
7oz can pitted black or
    morello cherries in syrup
1¾ tbsp superfine sugar
2 scoops vanilla ice cream

Ingredients for 4

½ cup all-purpose flour
1 egg, beaten
1¼ cups reduced-fat milk
1 tbsp sunflower oil, plus
    a little extra
15oz can pitted black or
    morello cherries in syrup
2¾ tbsp superfine sugar
4 scoops vanilla ice cream

15 minutes preparation
20 minutes cooking

1 Put the flour in a bowl and make a dip in the center. Add the egg and gradually blend in half of the milk. Whisk in the flour until smooth, then whisk in the remaining milk and the oil.

2 Add a little oil to a 10in clean, nonstick skillet. Rub around the skillet with a paper towel, then heat over a medium heat. Pour 3–4 tablespoons of batter into the skillet and tilt it to coat the skillet evenly.

3 Cook for about 1–2 minutes, until the underneath is light golden. Flip the pancake over and cook for about 1 minute, until golden. Repeat to make 4 (8) pancakes. Stack with nonstick parchment paper between the pancakes.

4 Heat the cherries and juice in a small saucepan with the sugar for 5 minutes until the sauce thickens slightly. Roll up and serve two pancakes on a plate with 1 spoonful of hot cherry sauce and scoops of ice cream.

Chocolate Zabaglione

Low Fat

This hot, sweet, foaming dessert is usually made with vanilla as a flavoring. Try this chocolate version as a treat.

Ingredients for 2

6 amaretti cookies
⅔ cup Marsala or
**   medium-sweet sherry**
1 tbsp cocoa powder, plus
**   a little extra**
the yolks of 3 large eggs
1¾ tbsp superfine sugar
a few decorative chocolate
**   shapes or leaves**

Ingredients for 4

12 amaretti cookies
1¼ cups Marsala or
**   medium-sweet sherry**
2 tbsp cocoa powder, plus
**   a little extra**
5 egg yolks
¼ cup superfine sugar
a few decorative chocolate
**   shapes or leaves**

5 minutes preparation
5 minutes cooking

1 Place 1 cookie in the base of 2 (4) glasses, then sprinkle over 1 (2) tablespoons of the Marsala or sherry. Put the cocoa, egg yolks, and sugar in a large bowl and then place over a pan of simmering water.

2 With an electric mixer, whisk the mixture until smooth. Gradually add the Marsala or sherry in small batches, whisking well after each addition.

3 Continue whisking for about 10 minutes, until the mixture becomes pale, thick, and foaming and has increased in volume.

4 Spoon the zabaglione into the glasses and dust the top of each with a little cocoa powder. Serve decorated with chocolate shapes with the remaining cookies.

Chocolate Bread & Butter Puddings

Family Favorite

Puffy, croissant layers, packed with sticks of chocolate make lovely little hot puddings.

Ingredients for 2

- **1 tbsp butter**
- **2 chocolate croissants or pains au chocolat**
- **1 egg**
- **5 tbsp milk**
- **6 tbsp light cream**
- **½ tsp vanilla extract**
- **1¾ tbsp superfine sugar**
- **4 tsp light-brown sugar**

Ingredients for 4

- **1¾ tbsp butter**
- **4 chocolate croissants or pains au chocolat**
- **2 eggs**
- **⅔ cup milk**
- **⅔ cup light cream**
- **1 tsp vanilla extract**
- **¼ cup light sugar**
- **8 tsp light-brown sugar**

10 minutes preparation

20 minutes cooking

1 Preheat the oven to 375°F. Thickly butter 2 (4) 2½-cup-capacity ovenproof dishes and place them in a small roasting pan.

2 Cut the chocolate croissants into ¾in-thick slices and arrange them, overlapping, in the dishes. Now beat the eggs, then whisk them together with the milk, cream, vanilla extract, and superfine sugar.

3 Pour the dessert sauce over the slices, then sprinkle the top of each with 2 teaspoons of light-brown sugar.

4 Pour boiling water into the pan to come halfway up the sides of the dishes. Bake for 20 minutes, until golden brown and firm.

Crunchy Peach Layer

Family Favorite

It's always worth storing blocks of frozen cream in the freezer, then you can make this creamy dessert from pantry ingredients without going shopping.

Ingredients for 2

7oz can peach halves in syrup
1 tbsp amaretto liqueur (optional)
²⁄₃ cup heavy cream
1oz amaretti cookies
1 tbsp toasted, slivered almonds

Ingredients for 4

14oz can peach halves in syrup
2 tbsp amaretto liqueur (optional)
1 cup heavy cream
2oz amaretti cookies
2 tbsp toasted, slivered almonds

10 minutes preparation
No cooking

1 Drain the peaches and roughly chop 2 (4) halves into small cubes. Place the remaining peaches in a food processor with 2 tablespoons of the syrup from the can and the liqueur if being used.

2 Process the peaches until smooth, then set aside. Whip the cream until it forms soft peaks. Roughly break the cookies into chunks.

3 Fold the cream and peach paste together, then fold in the chopped fruit pieces. Place the crushed cookies in the base of 2 (4) glasses.

4 Spoon the cream mixture over the cookies, then top with the slivered almonds. Serve immediately.

Cinnamon Toasts

Family Favorite

Serve this hot and tasty French toast for dessert or for a weekend brunch.

Ingredients for 2

4oz white, thick-sliced bread
1 egg, beaten
4 tbsp milk
½ tsp ground cinnamon
1 tbsp superfine sugar
1¾ tbsp butter
2 tbsp maple syrup

Ingredients for 4

8oz white, thick-sliced bread
2 eggs, beaten
8 tbsp milk
1 tsp ground cinnamon
2 tbsp superfine sugar
¼ cup butter
4 tbsp maple syrup

5 minutes preparation
4 minutes cooking

1 Cut the crusts from the bread, then cut the slices in half into triangles.

2 Beat the eggs, milk, and half of the cinnamon and sugar together. Quickly dip half of the bread into the egg mixture to coat it. Now melt half of the butter in a large, nonstick skillet.

3 Cook the slices in the butter for 2 minutes on each side until golden, then keep warm. Melt the remaining butter, dip the remaining bread, and cook as before.

4 Mix the remaining spice with the superfine sugar and sprinkle over the toasts. Drizzle over the maple syrup and serve immediately.

Caramel Fruit Fondue

Easy Entertaining

This dessert is fun to make and serve, and your guests will love dipping the fresh fruits into the warm caramel sauce.

Ingredients for 2

1 small, ripe mango
½ ripe pineapple
1 dessert apple
1 tbsp lemon juice

Toffee Fondue

2 tsp cornstarch
7oz can evaporated milk
⅓ cup soft, light-brown sugar

Ingredients for 4

1 ripe mango
1 small, ripe pineapple
2 dessert apples
2 tbsp lemon juice

Toffee Fondue

4 tsp cornstarch
14oz can evaporated milk
½ cup soft, light-brown sugar

15 minutes preparation
10 minutes cooking

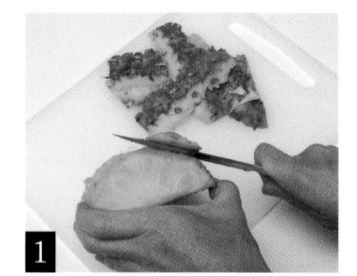

1 Cut the mango in half and cut away the pit, then peel the two halves. Cut the top from the pineapple, then cut away the peel and spines. Peel and core the apples.

2 Cut the prepared fruit into large 1in chunks. Toss the apple chunks in the lemon juice. Place a wooden toothpick in each piece and place on a large tray.

3 To make the fondue, blend the cornstarch to a paste

with 2 tablespoons of the evaporated milk. Place in a small nonstick saucepan and add the remaining milk and the light-brown sugar.

4 Heat, stirring, over a low heat until the sugar dissolves. Continue stirring over a medium heat for 10 minutes until the sauce thickens slightly. Pour into a bowl and serve on the tray, dipping each piece of fruit in the warm sauce.

Frozen Trifles

Family Favorite

Make these delicate, frozen sponge-cake trifles ahead of time. They are easy to serve topped with strawberries and chocolate sauce.

Ingredients for 2

2 trifle sponge cakes
2 tsp sweet sherry
4 heaped scoops vanilla block ice cream
2 strawberries, sliced

Chocolate Sauce

¼ cup chocolate, broken into pieces
1 tbsp butter
1 tsp maple syrup

Ingredients for 4

4 trifle sponge cakes
4 tsp sweet sherry
8 heaped scoops vanilla block ice cream
4 strawberries, sliced

Chocolate Sauce

½ cup chocolate, broken into pieces
1¾ tbsp butter
2 tsp maple syrup

15 minutes preparation
10 minutes cooking

1 To make the sauce, melt the chocolate, maple syrup, and butter together in a small saucepan over a very low heat, or in the microwave oven on low. Cool for 10 minutes, stirring. Meanwhile, clear a space on a freezer shelf and set the freezer to fast freeze.

2 Cut each trifle sponge cake in half horizontally into two layers. Place a sponge half on a small tray and sprinkle with ½ teaspoon sherry, then repeat with the remaining halves.

3 Soften the ice cream and spread in an oblong layer over one sponge cake. Shape into a block the size of the sponge base.

4 Place the remaining sponge layer on top and sprinkle with the remaining sherry. Freeze for 10 minutes until firm. Drizzle with chocolate sauce and serve topped with a strawberry fan.

Index

B

bakes
    Italian meatball and pasta — 57
    sizzling sausage — 45
    vegetable and cheese — 154
beef
    chili with red kidney beans — 60
    spaghetti Bolognese — 72
    steak with herby cheese sauce — 204
    Thai beef — 181
bruschettas — 103
burgers — 46
    bean — 153

C

cheese toasties — 94
chicken — 17
    and mango salad — 85
    Caesar salad — 97
    curry, rice, and peas — 62
    sauteéd chile breasts — 183
    spicy broil — 39
    spicy teriyaki — 119
    sticks — 65
    tandoori — 77
    Thai curry — 50
    with penne — 88
chili
    vegetarian — 132
    with red kidney beans — 60
chocolate
    banana splits with chocolate sauce — 217
    bread and butter puddings — 244
    custard bananas — 232
    microwave pudding — 221
    zabaglione — 243
cinnamon toasts — 248
curries
    cauliflower and potato — 131
    chicken, rice, and peas — 62
    Thai chicken — 50

D

dal, lemon — 162

E

eggs
    omelet, smoked ham, cheese, and chive — 106
    scrambled — 83

F

fish — 17
    and fries — 53
    crunchy cod pie — 66
    fusilli with salmon and garlic cream — 104
    ham and cheese broils — 59
    herby crusted — 171
    monkfish with oyster sauce — 198
    salmon steaks with lemon butter — 176
    sautéed sea bass with herbs — 201
    smoked-haddock and potato wedges — 48
    Thai fish cakes — 193
    trout fillets with shallot butter — 197
    tuna risotto — 91
frittata — 101
fruit — 18
    banana splits with chocolate sauce — 217
    broiled pineapple with caramel cream — 215
    caramel fruit fondue — 250
    caramelized oranges — 237
    cherry pancakes — 240
    chocolate custard bananas — 232
    crunchy peach layer — 247
    fruity toasts — 226
    lemon and kiwi-fruit layers — 238
    mangoes with Marsala cream — 222
    raspberry fluff — 225
    rhubarb and orange pots — 231
    strawberries with mascarpone — 235

G

gnocchi with tomato sauce — 147

H

herbs — 18, 22-3

I

ice cream — 17
    banoffee sundaes — 228
    frozen trifles — 253

K

kabobs	207

L

lamb	19
kabobs	207
kidneys with mushrooms	209
koftas	114
liver and bacon stir-fry	41
minted fillets	174
pesto -broiled chops	202

M

microwaves	30-4, 221

P

pasta	
cheesy leek	145
chicken with penne	88
Florentine	75
fusilli with salmon and garlic cream	104
Italian meatball bake	57
macaroni and cauliflower cheese	137
penne with broccoli	123
shrimp and lemon ribbons	210
spaghetti Bolognese	72
spaghetti with cherry tomatoes	81
tagliatelle with creamy bacon sauce	92
tricolor	157
with crab	194
pizzas	
French bread	109
Skillet	110
polenta with ratatouille	125
pork	19
chops with lima-bean mash	69
gingered fillet	169
lemon patties	116
meatballs with bean stew	43
with prunes	187
potatoes	34-5
baked, with frankurters and mustard sauce	70
cauliflower and potato curry	131
smoked-haddock and potato wedges	48

R

rice	19
curried chicken and peas	62
kedgeree, mushroom and bacon	113
mushroom risotto	128
prawn and vegetable risotto	189
Thai vegetable	143
tomato with kidney beans	149
tuna risotto	91

S

salads	
cannellini-bean and artichoke	140
chicken Caesar salad	97
couscous and fava bean	135
mango and chicken	85
Salade Niçoise	86
Thai beef	181
three-layer	158
two-bean	127
sausages	19
sizzling bake	45
shellfish	
pasta with crab	194
shrimp and lemon ribbons	210
shrimp and vegetable risotto	189
shrimp jambalaya	178
shrimp	18
shrimp and lemon ribbons	210
shrimp and vegetable risotto	189
shrimp jambalaya	178
soups	
bacon and bean minestrone	98
stews	
lima bean	165
pork meatballs with bean stew	43
skillet	54
stir-fries	
duck and honey	173
liver and bacon	41
vegetable	161

T

trifles	
frozen	253
tropical	219

credits & acknowledgements

The author would like to thank Denby (www.denby.co.uk), for supplying its china and cookware for purposes of photography, and Harrison Fisher and Co. (www.premiercutlery.co.uk), for supplying the knives and some of the small kitchen utensils used in the step-by-step photographs in this book. Thanks also to Vicki Smallwood, for her creative food-styling, and to photographers Colin Bowling and Paul Forrester, at Britannia Studios.